THE GRASS IS GREENEST WHERE I AM

Living in Your Own Love & Light
and Sharing Your Unique Gifts
with the World

NOAH CRANE

Published by:
Conscious Co-op
Boca Raton, FL 33428

ISBN:
Softcover: 978-0-69216-967-4
Hardcover: 978-0-57841-659-5

Cover and interior design: Gary A. Rosenberg
www.TheBookCouple.com

Because of you, I get to be me!

*To my amazing husband, Steven Crane,
my teacher, lover, and best friend.*

*You dance through life with incredible ease
that is so contagious.*

*Thank you for your unconditional love
and support, my sweet angel.*

Contents

Introduction

*No competition, no comparison, no scarcity.
I live in my own love and light and share
my unique gifts with the world.*

What if you thought of your life as a patch of grass? Your greenest patch of grass is attainable with regular watering, care, attention, and love. What if you did not compare your grass to any other grass, but instead decided to nurture your own gifts and talents? What if watering your grass daily with love, acceptance, patience, forgiveness, and care was just a way of life?

Many years ago, I made the decision to water and nurture my grass every day, and as a result, I have been able to live a much happier life. The decision to water my own grass shifted my life and made me grateful for all I have. There is no need for me to compare myself to others or worry about scarcity or compete with anyone else. The Grass Is Greenest Where I Am mindset has given me the strength to be present to the love that's abundant in my life daily. You can have the greenest grass, too . . . if you decide you can!

Your greenest grass does not come from ego. It comes from self-love, a love for your journey, and a love for others.

Watering your grass is self-acceptance, self-empowerment, and self-love. You can create your greenest grass when you no longer give your power away to others, when you believe in yourself, and when you are grateful for your life. Creating your greenest grass is about taking your power back and growing up, breaking old cycles that don't work and creating new ones that do, accepting yourself exactly where you are now, and clearly seeing your magnificence. This means never giving up on yourself, creating the life you seek, realizing the power of your words and thoughts, and using them to empower your life. Your words and thoughts create your world.

What if you choose to change the way you talk and think about life and re-create your life to be the way you want it to be? As adults, we have the power of choice. Your choices are important because they create your experiences. They are the very foundation of your life. When you have a strong foundation, you will be in a position to create anything you desire. You must carefully weigh your decisions, for whatever you choose becomes your reality. So be clear in your intentions and never settle for anything less. Mindful choices with clear intentions create new opportunities for manifesting everything and anything you desire. Always remember that you are the creator of your path and the navigator toward your destination in life. You must believe in yourself, be open, and be intentional with your choices. It's a simple formula for a lifetime of peace, gratitude, happiness, and love.

You are not a victim of your past circumstances. Rather, you are the creator of your story and you narrate your own experiences. You no longer buy into other people's experiences; rather you write your own. You choose the people in your life who truly love you and empower you. You create an inspiring life for yourself, and that begins by acknowledging that your grass is greenest exactly where you are.

The concept and belief that "the grass is greenest where I am" came from my own journey in life, some of which I will share with you throughout this book. I'm so grateful to be able to share this message with you, because it changed my life and my world. *The Grass Is Greenest Where I Am* is my story and approach to life, and it can be yours, too, if you decide that it will be. We can all create our own greenest grass and live in peace, love, happiness, and gratitude, no matter what we are going through or where our life is today, and no matter what challenges we are facing now. *The Grass Is Greenest Where I Am* will help you recognize that you have unique gifts in this world that you are meant to share with others and that you should believe in you!

I'm forever grateful for my ever-evolving journey. It does not stop the challenges, but it keeps me moving powerfully forward, open to receive and see the daily miracles that exist in me and around me. I'm honored that I was born with this message to share with you so that you can also stay empowered in your life journey. Once you decide "the grass is greenest where I am," life transforms—like a butterfly emerging from a chrysalis. Like a butterfly, you free yourself of any comparisons, release the need to compete, and let go of the idea that you aren't enough or that you don't have enough.

The Mantra "The Grass Is Greenest Where I Am"

Part of having the greenest grass is just declaring it. As soon as you declare it, you create a new reality for yourself and your life. When you say, "The grass is greenest where I am," you will believe it; it will become your truth. I created the mantra "The grass is greenest where I am" to empower my life as well as yours. By repeating these words, you are making the choice to be present in your life and nurture your special gifts with no comparison to others. It keeps you focused on learning to nurture your life daily and creating happiness and fulfillment now. You are no longer looking at other people's lives, thinking they have it better than you. This mantra keeps you empowered every day with the knowledge that you have the power to sustain a rich life of self-connection and self-love.

When you create the shift within yourself, the mantra "The grass is greenest where I am" changes the way you see your life and you become happy exactly where you are, which connects you to your peace, gratitude, and love. It keeps you moving in the right direction because you are less distracted by what others are doing and more focused on your own life journey.

The mantra "The grass is greenest where I am" appears throughout this book to deepen your connection to yourself. This is a journey of self-discovery and growth, so you can become the best version of you. It is not selfish to say, "The grass is greenest where I am." Rather it is an empowering affirmation to self-actualization and bliss. You can create your own greenest grass and live a life of connection and consciousness rather than a life of habit and self-sabotage. This is the work you came here to do, one day at a time, one step at a time, as you get closer to your true purpose in this life.

By the end of this book, you will have the tools to create your own greenest grass by applying the methods I have been using for years to help others see their own potential love and light. It is an honor to share my gift with you and help you on your journey to a self-fulfilling and abundant life.

1. I Create My Greenest Grass

I am blessed and supported
as I go through my journey.

How would your life look if you made a decision to notice that the grass is greenest where you are, no matter where you are in your life, how much money you have, or what challenges you are dealing with at this time? To discover how you can have the greenest grass, I invite you to answer the following questions:

❧ What if watering your grass daily with love, acceptance, patience, and forgiveness was just a way of life for you—so much a way of life that you did not have to think about it because it came naturally to you?

❧ What if you could always be happy for other people and vice versa and not be jealous or envious of other people's successes?

❧ What if love was present in all you did and said and exchanged?

❧ What if you felt complete, like nothing was missing in your life, because your life was so full of love and joy?

❣ What if you were no longer a victim of your life but the creator of everything you wanted?

❣ What if you stopped focusing on what is not working and created a world where there is love, balance, and harmony?

❣ Could you actually create your own future, your world, and your reality?

❣ Could you stop feeling stuck in your relationships, your ideas, and how you think things should be, and embrace life fully, with love and compassion, exactly where you are?

❣ Could you create everything you want with your thoughts and your actions?

It is your choice. *Everything* in life is a choice, and you create your life moment by moment. If you are the one who writes your own story anyway, it might as well be one you love. I am not suggesting that you will have control over everything that happens, but you *do* have control over your decisions, choices, attitudes, love, flow, kindness, compassion, and happiness.

Having the greenest grass is a decision you make for yourself and your life, just like being happy, joyful, and fun. All these decisions are up to you. You can create them every day at any time, no matter what is going on in your life. That's the power you have! You are so powerful that when you choose the path of creation instead of the path of your past, you will transform your life. When you are re-creating, you are leaving the past behind by shifting and changing your perspective.

This is your life, so you get to choose your words, thoughts, and actions. I have always done this, so I know that it is possible. Sometimes I do it subconsciously, and other times I do it consciously. I have always created everything in my life, from the amazing man I chose to marry to the kind of life I wanted to live. I get to choose the kind of people I have close to me. Having my life work the way I want it to work has always been my driving force. When you understand your own power, there is only one real choice, and that choice is to keep re-creating what you truly desire and want through commitment to yourself and your journey.

To create your greenest grass, you must water it often, love it a lot, and be grateful for all the gifts it has given you. When you truly feel the grass is greenest where you are, you are no longer comparing yourself to others—for example, your kids to other people's kids, your looks to other people's looks, and your possessions to other people's possessions. You are focusing on your own gifts and nurturing your own talents. You are grateful, content, and immersed in your own love of life. Your heart is so full of love that you have lots to give to others. You realize that this journey is full of choices, and you must use your power to create your path.

It's time to think bigger! Yes, anything is possible when you believe in yourself and your life.

No Competition

Okay, so you were the fastest sperm! Yes! You already won the lottery of life! Now it's time to chill and relax. When you put out the right energy, life will align with you and all that you are up to creating. No need to chase things that are not meant for you; that will only leave you empty, unfulfilled, and wanting more. It is not the first one who gets the prize, but rather the one who listens and is open to receive everything the universe/God has to give at the perfect time.

That brings me back to my younger years when I worked at a boutique in downtown Chicago. There were a few of us salespeople on the floor at one time. This was a very high-end boutique that sold clothing for thousands of dollars. When a new customer would walk in the door, one of the salespeople would immediately greet them. I decided to take a step back and not jump at the first customer who would walk through the door. I let the other salespeople go as they wanted and patiently waited for my turn.

It was interesting to see how things would turn out when I was not competing with anyone else. Somehow, I always got the right customers, the ones who were there to spend big money. I was a top salesperson, I believe, because I was open to receiving the right energy, rather than being in competition. I started to understand how my openness to receive was supporting me in my life. Competition does not make sense, for there is abundance for all when we change the way we think and start seeing the miracles all around us. I was not sitting on the couch doing nothing, but rather I was working toward my goals without competing with anyone else.

Our only competition should be with ourselves, not others. I compete with myself to be a better mom, wife, and friend, or to have a healthier lifestyle or body. I don't do it for anyone but me, so that I can feel good in my body and in my life. This is *my* journey; I want to fill it with love, peace, happiness, kindness, and abundance. Why would I strip it away or water it down with competition? All competition creates is stress, fear, lack, unhappiness, inferiority, and ego. Whatever we choose, we create ourselves, so why not choose connection over competition?

Competition will never give you a loving and fulfilling life. The only competition you should have is with yourself to be a better person than you were yesterday. You cannot be your best self when you are focused on competing with others. You are unique and must define yourself by your own and not others' standards. Choose to custom-create a life you love that supports you and your growth. Take the actions needed toward the things that inspire you most and fill your life with love, light, and joy. Be a leader on your path and get out of the rat race life has created by standing in your own beauty daily. No one can do this work for you; you are the creator and designer of your own life.

You were born for a reason:
to leave your impact on this world.

No Comparison

There is no reason to ever compare yourself to anyone else. You are unique, the only one of you in the world. It is time to turn the spotlight back on you and connect to your own love and light. Find your inside shine by connecting to it at every moment. This is your responsibility. The more you find connection to yourself, the more you can appreciate every moment. The more you can look inside yourself with love and gratitude, the more present you become to the miracles in your life. You learn to appreciate yourself, your own beauty and uniqueness, and the gifts you have been given. You realize that there is no reason to ever compare yourself to anyone else because doing so only causes you suffering. You can appreciate others' talents, beauty, and uniqueness without having to compare them to yours.

Comparison is a way of making things wrong in our own life and thinking someone else's life is better than ours. When you learn to connect to yourself rather than competing with others, you can always find happiness within you. When you can bring your true gifts out and share them with the world with passion, you bring excitement into your life and the lives of others.

You don't ever need to be like anyone else because you are you for a reason, a reason much bigger than you may even be able to see or understand right now. It is that constant nurturing of your life that will start shifting your perspective and open new opportunities for you that may not have been there before. Because everything starts with you, as you shift your mindset and thinking, you start changing your life. There is only one person you are responsible for, and that is you.

When you shift your thinking, you start to shift your life. Someone else's gift is not meant for you because that gift comes easily and naturally to them and is their true contribution to this world. Your gift is something no one can take away from you, for sharing it with the world is the reason you were born. You can never lose when you live your purpose—your true gift—for it was yours from the very beginning. Your job is just to uncover it by listening, being, believing, and taking actions to create your life.

Your gift is already within you, waiting for you to unwrap it. The journey is the unfolding and manifesting of the gift in order to share it with the world; it is learning to stand in your own love and light, without letting others dim your light or buying into the outside world, which is always pulling you in different directions. Learn to accept yourself exactly where you are with love and compassion. When you keep believing in yourself and nurturing your life, with no comparison to others, your light will keep shining brightly and new opportunities will always come your way.

You don't need all the answers right now, for it will all unfold at the perfect time when you are ready. Just remain open to receive the answers as they come. Find what lights you up and makes you truly happy. The better you know yourself, the closer you will come to living your true purpose.

If there are people in your life who always compared you to others when you were growing up, realize that you need to forgive them in order for you to be at peace. Find gratitude and compassion for yourself, knowing that you are forever a student of life and also a teacher of life. Share all that you know with others, and leave your mark on this world. You never need to be anything but you, and being you is perfect and enough. Be true to yourself and others by being authentic and loving as you walk through your journey. Release all doubts, fears, and comparisons. Learn to trust yourself and your journey. Without comparing yourself to anyone else, realize how truly amazing you are!

As I shift my inner world, I re-create my outer world. Anything is possible when I believe in Me.

No Scarcity

Have you ever heard someone say that they never have enough money? It seems like their words and thoughts keep creating exactly that reality for themselves. They are always in scarcity or lack, and they never have enough. Why do some people have so much and others so little? What is the difference between a wealthy person and a poor person? Poverty thinking keeps us in a cycle of scarcity that limits our capacity to receive abundance from the universe/God. Yes, sometimes people are blessed enough to have wealth passed down to them, but that is not the case for most of us.

What I realized over time is that what you believe and buy into is the very thing you create in your life. If you grew up with lack or scarcity, it may have shaped how you think and therefore may have become a part of your subconscious. It could be so deeply ingrained that you don't even realize you may have a part in creating it unconsciously. As life and others have proven time and time again, lack becomes a part of one's life and reality. It may be a cycle that you have participated in for years, so how could it not become your reality and truth?

When you buy into poverty thinking, you learn to think and play safe. You are constantly in a survival mode, living from paycheck to paycheck, day to day. If this is your reality, it is very hard to think and see things from a different perspective when such a perspective has not been revealed to you yet. You may feel stuck, unfulfilled, and afraid to try something new or may not know how to create a life you love. You set limits on yourself, and therefore life looks limited rather than limitless. You know there is more for you, yet your fears keep you stagnant. When you get stuck in the cycle of lack, your fears become your reality and you keep spinning your wheels without making any forward movement. It is a frustrating yet familiar place to be! I know; I have been there myself. I also know that the story of scarcity can change when you realize that the only limits you have are the ones you have put on yourself. Time and time again, when I released my attachment to fear and scarcity and trusted the journey ahead, I experienced ease and flow in life.

You have the power to put your fears aside and step into the unknown of your life. You do that first by changing your thinking from "I don't have enough" to "I have all that I will ever need." Just a change in how you think and speak starts shifting you in a new direction. Knowing you are always surrounded by abundance is as simple as adjusting your lenses so that you can see it. When you do, you are able to reach out and grab everything you want and need, knowing that endless power and possibility is always within you.

If you keep doing the same thing over and over again, you will always get the same results. Taking a new, forward step toward a new outcome or goal already starts creating that outcome. All you want and seek is within you when you stop limiting your thoughts and possibilities. You can only show up in life as great as you can imagine yourself to be. Imagination is a creative and powerful tool to start that shift toward what you desire. Some of us are early bloomers and others are late bloomers, but wherever you are now is the perfect time to start. I happened to be a late bloomer, and accepting that makes it empowering. The most important thing is that you get there eventually, no matter when you do, by learning to meet yourself exactly where you are with love, gratitude, and compassion. There is nothing wrong with where you are on your journey, unless you decide to see it that way.

Life unfolds at the perfect time—when you are ready and aligned with your path. Your job is to stay focused on the course and to be open to receive all the gifts this world has to offer. Most important is to keep believing in yourself and moving toward what you want to create. Don't let other people's opinions and beliefs crush you or your dreams. Remember that you are not like anyone else and be grateful for that, but stay connected to others because the power is always in connection, not in separation. Stay authentic and real and open to every moment of every day. This journey is not about the end result but rather about the love you spread along the way. Keep shining your light brightly, and the world will shine it back on you. When you do this, you will always have enough.

2. The Story of My Past

The grass is greenest where I am because I say so.
I am responsible for my own happiness
and creating my own life.

I was born in Israel in 1965, to a single mom who loved me with all her heart and soul and always wanted only the best for me. I was born on a kibbutz, which is a special community of a few hundred people who work toward a common goal, take care of each other, and share in the profits.

When my mom married my stepfather and decided to move to the United States in 1976, all my sense of security disappeared. Everything I knew changed in one moment; it felt like the carpet was pulled out from under me. All the family I knew and loved was gone, and I was just eleven years old. I no longer had the support of a community of adults and peers with whom I shared a common language and interest. I felt lost, unable to find stable ground or a foundation in my life.

We moved to Chicago, and I was put into the public school system. I did not receive much guidance or help. Inside, I was screaming for help, but no one heard me. I was shuffled around without counseling or support. The kids made fun of my name and my Jewish religion. I went to the public school only part of the day, and then was taken by bus to another school to learn English. I totally missed the part of the day where the other students learned science and math, so I fell very behind.

I started lying about my religion because I wanted acceptance. At home, things were turbulent as well. My stepfather was a controlling and abusive man. I had no voice in my home, and I was completely controlled by the adults around me. My stepfather called me names on a regular basis, and I ran away from home a few times. I did not know myself anymore. I was completely disconnected from the image I saw in the mirror. I was a sad child.

When I was fourteen, we moved to a better neighborhood. Still, I lived most of my life fearing that I was insignificant and small. I did not have many friends and felt rejected by most peers. A lost child, I was unable to focus in school, my home life was unbearable, and I felt that I had no power or voice.

However, I was stronger than I thought. There was an unseen spark of energy and strength, light. I would not just stand there and take the abuse. I was a fighter inside. I grew up with a big poster of Albert Einstein above my bed. It read, "Great Spirits have always encountered opposition from mediocre minds." Those words, which always made sense to me, kept me focused on what really mattered, an idea that was even bigger than me at that time.

At age fifteen, as I was lying in bed, feeling sad and realizing I had no control over anything, I had an awakening I will never forget. I realized that my childhood would not last forever and I would someday be an adult. When that time comes, I would make my own choices and decisions and take back my power and control. I decided in that moment that, although I hadn't chosen this terrible childhood, my adulthood would be amazing because I would create the life I wanted to live by making the right choices for me. I made that commitment without knowing how it would manifest; I simply trusted it would! I put that possibility in my future.

After public school, I went to college, but I still lived at home. I couldn't focus or study in my home environment, so eventually I dropped out. At age nineteen, I joined the Israeli army to get away from home. I was so desperate to find a safe place to call home and establish a connection to myself, but I couldn't find myself—or my place in the world—anywhere. I had countless boyfriends in my twenties because I was looking for love in all the wrong places. When my service in the army was over, I returned to the United States, still searching for love and a safe place to call home.

One day, I had a chance to read a great book that changed my life forever: *You Can Heal Your Life* by Louise Hay. After I read it, I felt more empowered, and life started to make sense. I saw myself differently, with more compassion, forgiveness, and love. I knew I had a lot of growing up to do, and I knew I wanted change. I felt desperate and hungry for knowledge and self-growth. In my late twenties, in the midst of dating uncommitted men, I decided to take my life into my own hands. I remembered the promise I'd made to myself a decade earlier: I would take back my power and control. I wanted a partner who saw my inner beauty, not just my outer shell. I wanted to find my soul mate. I was ready to choose rather than be chosen.

That day was a turning point in my life. I took back my power and bravely stood in that power, a choice that changed my life forever. I was no longer the victim of my past, but rather the creator of my future. I realized that we are all creators of our life, and we can write a new story that empowers us any time we choose. My greenest grass had sprouted.

Your life didn't change; you changed.
Keep transforming yourself
to create a life you love.

3. Choosing the Right Partner

Soul connection is the key
to an uplifting relationship.

If you decide you want to have a life partner, the partner you choose is by far the most important decision you will ever make in creating your greenest grass. When you partner with someone, you and your partner become one unit rather than two people on two different paths. Partnering with the right person is the difference between being happy most of the time and being happy half or less than half of the time.

A partner is your support system, your cheerleader, your friend, your lover, your foundation in life. Having the right partner makes the difference between being uplifted versus being put down or ignored. This choice cannot be left up to chance or to love alone. Just because you love someone does not mean that person is right for you. I decided I would never settle, no matter how long it took. I was a grown woman and a seeker of growth and transformation. I knew I had the power to choose, and I did not have to give it away anymore.

The more I spoke to people, the more I understood what I was looking for. I was working at a hair salon at that time, as an assistant. One day, a client came in who made a profound difference for me. As we were talking, she said, "Noah, I have been married for thirty years now to an amazing man who ADORES me. Find a man who adores you! If he adores you now, he will adore you thirty years from now."

Adore? I thought. Adoration seemed like a foreign language to me. I had never had a man adore me before. I was not a mom yet, but the word "adore" impressed me as such a powerful word that it could only be reserved for the love a mother has for her child. I didn't realize I could have that in a romantic relationship. I was grateful for the message and decided I deeply wanted an adoring life partner.

To choose the right partner, I created a game to keep me empowered, on track, and able to move efficiently forward toward my goal. I was determined to find my soul mate and create the life I had always desired. The Elimination Game was born.

There were certain guidelines I would follow. I would not go out with the same man more than three times unless it was leading to something serious; I had no time to waste on fancy dinners and small talk now. I had to stay focused on what I wanted to create. I would not be afraid to tell him what I wanted, which was to find my soul mate and start a family. I would not get upset if he walked away in fear because that would mean he was not the right man for me. I knew that when the right man stood in front of me, there would be nothing I could say or do that would be wrong because it would be right. I intended to have fun eliminating the wrong ones to find that one special man who would adore me, who would appreciate me for my inner beauty instead of just my outer beauty.

This Elimination Game was fun, lighthearted, and empowering. I often say, as women, we wear our hearts on our sleeve; we are ready to give our heart away before a man actually shows us with his actions, not words, that he deserves it. We then wonder why we get so hurt when we discover he doesn't deserve or value our heart. You must *never* give your heart away so quickly. A man should show you that he deserves your heart with his actions, not his words, before you should even consider trusting him with your most valuable possession. Keep your eyes wide open and see what you are *really* getting. I was not leaving anything to chance, for I was now the creator of my future life.

I played the Elimination Game for three months, and then it happened: I met Steve.

It is a beautiful story, one that must be told. My twenty-two-year-old sister, Ayelet, was getting married. She is eight years my junior and was getting married first. She had met her now-husband, Avraham, through a matchmaker in New York. I was thirty years old and living in Chicago at the time and in the process of playing the Elimination Game.

I flew to New Jersey for the engagement party. I walked into a beautiful, warm home, so full of love and happiness. And there he was—Steve. Our eyes met, and we started to talk. That evening, he asked me if I wanted to go see a movie or if I'd like to walk in the rain. I chose to walk in the rain so we could get to know each other better. During our walk, I opened up about what I wanted and so did he. We spent the weekend together, surrounded by celebration, family, and love. Steve was in dental school at the time in Boston and had also flown in for the special day. You see, Steve and Avraham are brothers. The entire weekend was magical. We spent as much time together as possible.

I had a flight back to Chicago on Sunday. Steve asked me to stay for another couple of days and paid to extend my ticket. We even joked about going to the mall to look for engagement rings. We were like two kids, fearlessly jumping into the deep side of the pool headfirst. Being together was easy. Steve is loving, fun, sweet, gentle, a beautiful soul—being with him was like nothing I had felt before. My dreams were coming true, and I knew my Elimination Game had a lot to do with it.

We had a long-distance relationship in the beginning. We spoke on the phone day and night, getting to know each other even more. Two weeks after we met, Steve came to Chicago to see me for the weekend, which showed initiative and positive action on his part. Two weeks after that, he came to Chicago again, but this time with an engagement ring. One month from the day we met, I had a ring on my finger. What a blessing!

The action Steve took and the love he showed me was exactly what I wanted in my life—the real deal, my soul mate. Our love did not stand on empty promises or just words; it was and still is deeply rooted in real, unchanging, adoring love. For the first time in my life, I understood what it meant to adore and be adored. I am forever grateful for this journey and the choices I made because they brought me to him!

When you place yourself in a position of self-love and believe in your greatest self, you won't settle for less than you are worth or for less than what you truly want: someone who will cherish and believe in you, too. The key is to believe with all your being that you are worth that and eliminate anything that falls short of your vision and dreams.

Steve is my best friend in the whole world. He is so sweet, kind, loving, and supportive of me. He is an amazing father to our beautiful children, completely committed to our family and our love. We have been married now for over twenty years. Our love just keeps growing and is stronger today than ever.

STEVE'S PROPOSAL

My soul loves your soul sooooo much!

"My darling angel, you are the love of my life. From the special moment you came into my life, I became a complete man. The awesome miracle of you has created within my life and my future a series of smaller miracles, rippling through me like an electric shock wave, creating happiness and good fortune at every turn. You are a unique and special person, a true gift from God whom I shall treasure always. Darling Noah, I cannot bear to live without you, and if you will have me, I will be honored to be your husband and blessed if you would be my wife. Noah, will you marry me?"

"I do, I do, I do! I love you, Steven!"

4. The Power of Connection

When we share our challenges, it gives us a chance to cultivate a deep connection and appreciation for each other.

Life is not meant to be lived alone! We all need each other's support and love to succeed in this world. I often say to my husband, "Because of you, I get to be me." Whether you are married or not, other people's support makes it possible to be who you are meant to be in this world. No one can live life successfully by themselves. We all need each other on this journey to help lift each other's souls and spirits.

Who is it in your life that helps support you to be your very best? Who gave you the wings so that you could fly higher in this life? Bringing awareness to your supporters brings more gratitude into your everyday life. We all must realize the impact we have on each other and the responsibility to help one another to grow and evolve. When we help others, it helps us energize our own strengths and lives. Together we are much more powerful than we are when we are alone. When we help others, we are getting out of our own head and sharing our love and light with them. In return, they shine their light on us, which strengthens our soul and enhances our own journey.

You see, we are all mirrors. I am you, and you are me. Everything you do for others reflects back into your life and helps you move forward. When you realize the strength of togetherness, you can be certain that anything is possible with the right connections. Everyone has something to share with you, whether it is wisdom, an idea, a helping hand, or advice to help guide you toward your goals and dreams. The world needs you to share your gifts; the expression of your gifts comes through others. Some connections are temporary, others can be longer lasting, and some last a lifetime, but they are all valuable. These connections are all here to support you and for you to support and/or learn from them.

As you go about your daily life, you meet all kinds of people, and everyone has their own journey, struggles, and triumphs. Yet we are all seeking more love and light in our lives. You can only be responsible for yourself and what you do on a daily basis. To have more love and light in your life, give your light and love freely so that it is mirrored back at you. Your reflection of light on others will help them shift their lives while you shift yours. It is a beautiful thing when we can all be responsible for how we show up in the world. Life is not about what you can get, but what you can give. When you give, you get back much more than you can imagine.

I always turn on my inner light before I leave my house. Like flipping a light switch, I make a conscious decision to turn it on. I understand my power of love and light, and I know I can wrap each person I meet with it. It energizes me, gives me a purpose, and helps me feel grateful daily. I notice how much people are starving for light and love in their lives, and I have a deep desire to share mine with them. In return, I live surrounded by love and light because of the strength and love they share with me.

Realize the power of connections in your life. The blessing is found in each other when you share your love and light on a daily basis.

AN EXAMPLE OF BEING THERE FOR ONE ANOTHER

Our job as people is to get out of our own way, get out of our own heads, and be there for one another. We all need each other to rise and become who we need to be in this world. As you help others rise higher in their lives, you're also helping yourself rise. At times, we go through similar challenges or even the same challenges. This is a perfect opportunity to take action and support one another.

For example, in Florida, we sometimes experience hurricanes and need to prepare before they come. People often get into scarcity mode and hurricane supplies can sometimes be hard to find in the stores. Thanks to social media, as well as neighborhood communities, you can reach out to others and see if they have any resources to share with you. You can also share information and supplies with them. People need help putting up shutters or plywood, which can be a challenging job. Knowing that we can count on each other makes the challenge that much easier to tackle. Many bonds are forged in the face of difficult circumstances when people share their love and light with each other in this way.

No one can do it alone; together we are "won."

5. Commitment to Partnership and Family

A strong daily commitment to your
goals helps create your dream life.

We put a lot of energy into our career, our children, our pets, our social life, our obligations, our hobbies, and so on. The areas we nurture typically work well for us. But, for some reason, as time passes, we begin to take our intimate relationships for granted, and we think they will continue to work automatically. We often neglect the very thing that is most important to our well-being and happiness: our relationship with our significant other.

We don't make time to connect with, laugh with, love, appreciate, and play with one another. Our romantic relationships are the fertile soil we must nurture to grow our best life. Our partnerships should provide stability, security, and a soft place to fall. Nurturing one another must be our top priority, yet so often it is not.

A true partnership gives your life stability and a foundation of love to build upon. Guard your relationship like it is the most valuable treasure you have, realizing that if you are not moving energy toward what is important and are not present for one another daily, then that connection may weaken.

Our time gets consumed by many other things, like work, children, friends, and hobbies, and we soon forget to water our grass where it matters most. Without your focus and attention, you cannot expect all aspects of your life to work smoothly. You cannot sustain happiness or love without being proactive in those areas. It all starts with you and your priorities and commitments. Being in a beautiful, loving, healthy relationship nurtures your heart and soul daily. You keep one another supported, loved, joyful, and happy as you walk through your life journey together. To be loved, adored, and cherished is the biggest gift in life, one that is not easily replaceable. Finding time to connect, hug, laugh, love, and play is the key to long-lasting happiness.

The right love for you will evolve into a greater, deeper love over time. It is about a soul connection, a deep soul love that can never be broken. Find time each day to thank your soul mate for all they do and all they are. Make sure they know how much you love and appreciate them. Plan dates, time together to connect, share, and love. Don't look outside your relationship for fulfillment and love; find it within one another. Don't be blinded by the glitz and glamor of life. Stay focused on what really matters: your partner and your family. If you look outside yourself for fulfillment, you will always have a void in your core because external things will not bring you real happiness and love.

You have chosen your family and your partner for a reason. The souls with whom you choose to surround yourself are in your life for a reason. Don't push them away; instead, learn to nurture their very beings and cherish them. Their presence in your life will help you grow and become a better version of yourself. They will help you become more accepting, caring, and loving, and less judgmental and stuck in your own opinions and way of being. They are here to help you expand yourself to new heights. Be open and grateful, with an open mind, heart, and soul.

SUCCESS TAKES PRACTICE

Michael Jordan didn't get to be one of the best basketball players of all time by playing once a week! We tend to work harder for our careers than our personal relationships—which often need the most intensive work! Our relationships need time and dedication just as much, if not more, than our careers to be successful. We must play at our relationships daily.

6. Put Hearts Everywhere

Whatever we put out comes back to us.
When we choose love, we live in love.

I truly believe that whatever you put out in the world comes right back to you. That's why I put "hearts" everywhere. What I mean is that I shine my light and love on everyone I come into contact with. If you are constantly gossiping, competing with others, putting others down, and being unforgiving, you are only hurting yourself. I see energy as moving in a circle, and all you do comes back to you. All you are and all you do either helps you rise and create more light or creates more darkness and obstacles.

The world is round, and energy moves in a circular pattern around us at all times. You have to be intentional and mindful with what you want to create in this lifetime. By being intentional, you are responsible for your actions and the results you manifest as a result of those actions. The happier you are for others and the more love and light you spread by supporting others, the more happiness, light, and love will come back around to you.

The secret to having what you want is to also help others get what they want. You will start realizing that everything is connected when you become aware of this circular pattern of life. Your thoughts and your actions can either support you or be obstacles to moving forward. You can get closer to the life you desire when you mirror it out into the world. Be mindful of the energy you send to others because they are a part of you, and whatever you want to receive, you have to give. You cannot have love and peace if you are in chaos.

As you seek to grow and lead a more fulfilling life, you become more free-flowing in every aspect of your life. You give what you want to receive, consciously and openly. The hearts you put out will always come back to you tenfold.

Creating a world of love,
peace, and kindness is
our greatest hope
for the future.

7. Letting Go of Opinions and Beliefs

Our opinions and beliefs won't change
the world, but our love and connection will.
Together we are "won."

We know the age-old debate over toilet paper: Should it unwind from the top or the bottom of the roll?

Everyone has some strong opinions about how certain things should be done. Our opinions are strong, rooted, and embedded deep in our subconscious. After all, we'd been conditioned our entire childhood to see the world a certain way. We are so conditioned that often we don't even realize we are conditioned. I always say, in most cases, the apple does not fall far from the tree—in other words, we only know what we saw at home when we were growing up to be the truth, and it is upon those beliefs we lay the foundation for our lives. Even though we claim we will never do things the way our parents did, no one showed us how to do them differently. So, in most cases, we follow in our parents' path. However, those of us who are committed to growing and evolving beyond what we learned at home, in school, and from friends and other influences can *always* find a way to transform our lives.

One of our biggest challenges is to untangle ourselves from ourselves. It is not easy! We are often stuck in our way of thinking and being. We keep ourselves in bondage without even knowing that we're doing so. Our opinions and beliefs keep us from our own happiness, freedom, and well-being. We've lost our freedom without even knowing that we've lost it.

When you are able to let go of your opinions and are open to another way of thinking and seeing things, life becomes lighter and easier. You start to untangle and free yourself from the heaviness you are carrying. Trying to be right all the time creates heaviness. I would rather be happy than always be right. I would rather spread happiness to people than make them feel wrong. I would prefer to inspire and lift another soul by adding light to their life, rather than add to their darkness or mine.

We can all be a source of love and light for one another. Yet our opinions, limited thinking, and lack of flexibility and compassion can cause separation and competition between us. We must be the light we want to see in the world. When your opinions and beliefs become your only truth and way of doing things, you start seeing others as worth less than you. You are no longer connected to the whole. You cannot reach your own greatness without the support and love of others! We all need each other to rise up to our greatest potential because we are all one.

To grow, release any thoughts and beliefs that are

weighing you down and keeping you from being open to growth. As you release your way of thinking and your strongly held opinions of "the right way," life becomes lighter, happier, more peaceful, and fun.

GETTING OLDER & GROWING WISER

The best part of getting older is growing wiser and evolving into a greater version of who we are. As we grow and evolve, we can be better examples to the younger generation, who are also on their own journey of growth and transformation. We have a big responsibility to teach them how to turn on their light, grow, and transform. They are always looking to us for direction, guidance, and support. Their future depends on us, and we must learn to be the teachers they wish to follow.

8. The Power Is Within You

Everything you want is inside you already; your job is to uncover it by peeling back the layers of your life to expose more love and light.

In the movie *The Wizard of Oz*, Dorothy wants to go home to her family, but she does not know how to get back to them. On her journey, she meets friends who help her along the way. All throughout her journey she wears the ruby slippers, which have the magic power to send her home, yet she does not realize she has that power. Her story reminds me of our story, of our endless power, our need for connections, and our limited vision at times. Dorothy's story holds many great lessons for all of us.

Think of the story you tell yourself, even one that no longer affects you in your everyday life or in a given moment. That story can keep you less present and aware of your current situation and power. Your story is rooted in the past, yet chances are you play it in your head like it is happening right now. You may somehow lose track of your purpose and path because that story is still affecting you.

You may always be searching for the answers outside yourself, even though the answers are inside you at all times. How can you start seeing things more clearly and be more connected to yourself so you can see that the answers and solutions are always inside you, enabling you to create the life you desire? Your connection to yourself is crucial to changing your life. Everything you desire has to first start with you. When you put your energy into yourself, you can manifest all you want in the outside world. However, knowing that doesn't always cause an immediate shift. You need others to empower you and shine their light on you. The right connections will give you strength, direction, and hope to keep moving forward on your path and believe in your own power and light.

Recognize your limited vision and that you may not have a complete picture at this time. That's where you need to learn to have faith and trust in yourself and your journey. The only limits you have are the ones you believe you have because whatever you believe becomes your truth and reality. You discover your power by peeling away the old layers and creating something new. This is not easy to do, but it is definitely possible when you are committed to yourself and never give up on yourself. Giving up is not an option!

Trust that you are supported and loved along the journey and that all you want to create is just waiting for you to uncover it. There is nothing wrong. There are no mistakes. It is all just part of your growth and transformation. You must go through certain challenges and circumstances as you uncover your true power and gifts. You must write a new story to start changing your current situation. When you do that, you will shift and create all you want one step at a time—with love, patience, and commitment toward yourself and your life. You have a lifetime to shift and change, always moving forward.

So, what story are you telling yourself right now that is keeping you stuck in your past? What limitations do you believe you have that stop you from complete self-expression in the world? What is it that you are willing to give up today to create the life of your dreams? No matter what you do, there is always a cost and a payoff. What is it costing you to not be living your dream right now?

For me, not being able to get my message out was costing me my self-confidence, happiness, and self-worth, and it left me feeling stuck and not creative. I had to change and give up certain things that were keeping me stagnant, and the first change I made was getting out of my own head and my past story. That story kept me limited, fearful, and unable to share myself with the world. I had to stop hiding and isolating myself and playing small. I had to learn to use my voice and share my message, knowing it was important to share. I had to trust that the right people would connect with me and see my light and love. First I had to see it within myself.

You have to learn to get out of your own way to start creating a new path. You must reconnect with your power and light before change can occur outside for you. Find the connection between your mind, body, and soul so there is harmony and peace in all that you are and all that you do. Others can help you and support you, but the real work has to be done by you and you alone. No one can hand you change; change has to come from within.

You have probably heard the saying, "You can lead a horse to water, but you cannot make him drink." This means you can only create change in your life and not anyone else's. You must be ready and open to receive the gifts the universe/God has to offer you. Everything happens at the perfect time when you are open to receiving and giving freely of yourself.

The more you give, the more you will receive and the more you will become an open vessel for connection and love. The more people's lives you shift and touch, the more your own life can shift and open. You are no longer just being impacted by the world; you are causing an impact on the world. You start to feel lighter, as you realize you are only responsible for yourself and your own behavior, light, and love. You will notice that when you are connected to your light and love, everything and anything is possible. That's why that connection to yourself is so important to shifting the external parts of your life. You shift much faster when you surround yourself with people who believe in you and see your shine. Others are here to support you and that's why it's important to learn from them as well.

We all need to be a beacon of light for each other on this journey. As we shine our light on each other, we ignite each other's lives to shine even brighter on the world. Our energies can feed off each other to help create a transformed world of peace and love for all. We find the right connections by learning to choose the people we spend time with wisely. Those choices should not be taken lightly, for they can shift our perspective and our lives for the better. Consider whether the people in your life are building you up (like the Scarecrow, Tinman, and Lion), or bringing drama and chaos into your space (like the Wicked Witch and her flying monkeys). Your space on this journey is important and sacred; you don't want to clutter it with draining energies. Otherwise, you will always be taking a few steps back for every few steps forward, which is counterproductive. It's important to keep moving forward to live the life of your dreams.

You and you alone are responsible for your space, your happiness, your dreams. You must connect to the flow of the path—that yellow brick road you can follow toward your goals and dreams. It may be scary at times, but your faith will keep you strong and your trust will keep you going in the right direction. And, yes, there will be a prize at the end of that beautiful story. You will come to realize that you are living the life of your dreams with power and intention. You stepped into your power and never looked back because the past will never get you where you want to go or give you the life you want.

YOUR COLOR PALETTE

When you're fully expressed in the world, you get to paint the world in many different colors. You have a full palette to choose from when you are no longer stuck in the cycle of fear and hopelessness.

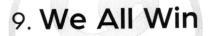

9. We All Win

We rise by empowering others to rise.
Everything we do has a direct
connection back to us.

I always say, "Together we are 'won,' and together we win!" When I win, you win, and when you win, I win. This is because we are one; we are all connected. I love the human race. I think we are amazing and have the potential to contribute positively to this world. As we evolve, we are better able to connect to our compassion, love, vulnerabilities, commitments, and connections, which is so inspiring to me. We have the extraordinary ability to express ourselves in a way that no other animal can. I am proud to be human, with all my vulnerabilities, doubts, self-love, self-sabotage, growth, and transformation. Yes, we are complicated.

As I walk through this journey, I know that everything is here to teach us something and help us grow. We are here to evolve, not to stay the same forever. I realize that growth is not easy since we are usually a direct image of our upbringings (what we saw and who we connected to during our informative years). Usually it's our family, friends, and life experiences that shape how we see the world today.

We all see the world through c⟍
lenses. Our life experiences have shap
thoughts, our ideas, our feelings, wha
taught—everything. We actually becom
many ways, not realizing that we are on a⟍
Your responses, your triggers, your actio⟍   ⟍ur
thoughts are mostly a result of how you expe ⟍nced life
up to this point. Breaking that cycle takes a lot of hard
work and the willingness to do better and evolve. It is not
easy to change after being stuck in others' perceptions
and ways of being for so long. It takes a real commitment
to yourself to actually start shifting who you are and finding others to help you grow and change.

I am grateful for the many amazing people who came
before me and paved the way for me and others on this
journey. I believe the most important thing is to never
give up on yourself and always know there are answers
out there, in everything and everyone, and that choosing
to be happy is your responsibility. You are paving the way
now for today's children and future generations to come.
You have a big responsibility to make the world better
for them!

It is so important to realize that habits are so hard, but
not impossible, to change, and that you must persevere,
no matter how many times you think you have failed. There
is no failure; there is only growth and lessons. Everyone
you meet can contribute to your growth and development,
and you can contribute to theirs. When you help others
do better in their lives, you are actually helping yourself
grow. I call it "lifting the souls." When you lift another's
soul, you help them see more clearly the greatness within

ves. You are helping them by sharing your light and love with them, thereby helping them tap into their own love and light. You are helping them see past where they are stuck, and realize their true self, not the story they made up about themselves. When you help others see their true potential, you are actually realizing your own true potential, and in return, they are now lifting your soul.

There is such an unseen connection of energy between you and the person you are helping that it actually changes both of your lives. As we become teachers to others and help them along the journey, they become teachers to us and others they encounter. Like a domino effect, we start shifting consciousness in the world. When I win, you win, and we all win, for we are all connected to one another and to the energy of our world. We create wholeness, harmony, and balance together, and therefore the world can shift and change for the better.

Love and light shared between us grows an abundant and beautiful garden of hope.

10. Surround Yourself with People Who See Your Shine

Love yourself enough to surround yourself with people who fill your heart and nurture your soul.

Real and authentic connections are deeply rooted in love. They are solid and grounded and help you feel empowered. They are not shallow or based on just feelings or one's own needs. Those relationships make all people involved feel loved and understood, and they add more joy, peace, and happiness to all our lives. They give us roots to grow and become our very best.

The ones who truly love you accept you just the way you are. They are not constantly judging you, but rather empowering you. I'm not talking about family now, but the friends we choose. When I was ready to choose my husband, many men were interested in dating me, but was it for the right reason? I did not want to be just another trophy they collected along the way. I wanted someone who could see past my outside and into my inside soul—my inner beauty, my love, my heart, my light and shine. I wanted someone who would dig deeper and see the real Noah.

When I told one guy I was dating that I couldn't see him anymore, he actually said that he would not get a chance to date someone as pretty as me again. That's not what I wanted to hear! It was clear to me that he was missing the things I was looking for most in a partner. I knew the outside was temporary, but the inside was the real gift. I focused on that when I was looking for my soul mate and husband.

You need laser focus to start shifting your life toward the right direction. You must keep your eye on the ball so you can catch it when it comes. You must learn to be open but cautious when choosing others to be a part of your life. Take a step back and watch their actions instead of listening to their words. Anyone you bring into your life can also bring problems and chaos. In this case, I believe less is more. Find people with similar paths, values, and hearts, people who are focused on the good rather than the bad. They should have a positive outlook on life and want to grow, be better, and do better. Seek friends who are honest, authentic, and want the best for you, friends who see your shine!

Don't rush into a friendship, but take your time building a bond through experiences together. It comes down to building a solid foundation over time, which is always the key in any friendship or relationship. Don't look for friends to fill a void in your life because then you become desperate and you can misjudge their intentions. Hold yourself in a high space of self-love always! Don't try to fit in with others or climb down to be on their level. If they are the right friends, they will meet you where you are.

Steer clear of drama and gossip and people who are addicted to it. Enough drama and chaos happens naturally in life without us looking for it! You get to choose, and whatever you choose will become your reality. Choose mindfully, for you are the navigator of your life. "If it doesn't flow, let it go." The right friendships and relationships should not be difficult to attain. It should be easy, effortless, and fun, fulfilling when you are in the company of the people you chose to be in your life.

Mindful choices, combined with elimination, will help you choose the right friends for you. I always say "You make your bed and then you sleep in it," so take your time choosing because your choices will either empower or disempower you. It's your responsibility to choose wisely and create a life you love.

Don't let "energy-drainers" suck you dry. Choose empowering connections full of love and light. The right connections energize us and help us rise higher than we thought we could.

11. Be Like Water

*Have faith that if it is meant to be,
it will flow easily like water.
Connect to the flow of life and be open
and flexible to change direction when
needed. You are supported and guided.*

Imagine you are opening a faucet of water and seeing how easily and effortlessly it flows down. Can you be more like water? Can you learn to move smoothly in your life in a steady steam, moment by moment and day by day? You will be happiest when you flow.

Imagine your breath flowing through your body and how vital it is for your life. As the breath moves through your body, consciously, you are able to attain calmness and balance. The flow of breath keeps you grounded and connected to yourself. The more it flows, the calmer you feel and the more in control you are. Flow starts with the connection to your breath. You may notice that when you are angry, you hold your breath and therefore block your ability to flow.

Imagine yourself in heavy traffic. You feel stuck with nowhere to go, and maybe you feel frustrated, powerless, and angry—there is no flow. A lack of flow brings out these emotions inside you. Now imagine that you are on a beautiful island on vacation, you have your day planned, and you are flowing easily from one activity to the next. You feel happy, excited, relaxed, peaceful, and joyful. Now imagine having that flow all the time, even in heavy traffic. It is that flow that keeps you happy and alive.

Everything in life has a flow that is constantly moving forward, ever changing, and evolving. Nothing ever stays the same. The key to happiness is learning how to shift yourself as life shifts, shedding things that hold you back from flowing and that no longer create happiness, peace, and love in your life. Even in our relationships, it is important to choose ones that flow easily and are flexible enough to shift with the changes. A relationship should not be a roller-coaster ride or a struggle! When things are meant to be, they will flow easily, with love and kindness. If it's not flowing, it is most likely going to cause you heartache, pain, and heaviness. I always say, "If it doesn't flow, let it go."

Your relationships should be the easiest part of your life since you get to choose them and create them yourself. Remember, everything is created by you and then you get to live in the reality you created.

Life can flow easily and much more gracefully if you choose the people you surround yourself with wisely. It is a conscious choice you get to make that will affect the rest of your life and your happiness. To me, there is nothing more important than our choices. We have the power to manifest and create our own happiness. How cool is that— that we are the creators of our flow and destiny in life? Learn to trust yourself by connecting to your intuition, the universe's guidance, and self-love. Standing powerfully for yourself and your life with faith and trust in this journey makes it all worthwhile. Sometimes jumping in headfirst when you know it is safe is okay. Sometimes backing up because the flow is just not there is okay, too.

As you create your life minute by minute, day by day, you are able to flow into your greatest self with fulfillment in your soul and love in your heart. You know you are guided and supported on this amazing journey. You are grateful to be able to flow like water. It is the only constant place of joy and connection to all that you desire. You therefore receive a fresh outlook on every day without taking anything for granted, for everything is a gift—even heavy traffic!

The attitude of gratitude
keeps us present
to the everyday miracles
we encounter.

12. Feelings Are Like the Wind

Realizing that feelings can change from one moment to another, let them flow and then let go.

Being connected to yourself and your feelings is very important. Notice how you feel, how you move through life, and the things that bring you joy and the things that don't. Feelings can be a great way to monitor yourself and your intuition. Your feelings can also let you know if something does not feel good or right and bring awareness to a situation you may want to avoid. However, feelings can be tricky as well when they become a driving force in your life by taking you away from your ambitions, intentions, dreams, and hopes.

Since feelings can change minute by minute, hour by hour, and day by day, they are not always a reliable source for making decisions. If you follow your feelings at all times, they can bring you to a place of unproductivity, unavailability, unhappiness, boredom, depression, hopelessness, helplessness, and so on. When your feelings become the reality of who you are at every moment, they can distort your truth and blind you from seeing your path. You cannot live life through feelings. Feelings are not always the truth; sometimes they might be your truth for just that moment and can keep you stuck if you don't let them go when they are no longer true.

I compare feelings to the wind. As the wind blows in one direction one moment and another the next, so do our feelings. Feelings are not stable or concrete or always reliable; they can be like riding on a roller coaster. You can never create true happiness or stability while you are on a roller-coaster ride.

You need to create a real path of growth and transformation with a strong foundation in order to build your life. You get that foundation not from your feelings, but from your actions. Actions are a true commitment to yourself and to your life. It did not matter how I felt when my kids woke up in the middle of the night and needed me. Of course, I felt like sleeping, but it was my responsibility to get up and take care of them, regardless of those feelings. My feelings would never get the job done.

Your feelings alone will take you out of the game or get you stuck within yourself rather than move you forward, flowing toward what you want to create. If you want to be happy, your actions, rather than your feelings, will help create the fulfillment and joy you seek. You are the creator of your path, and you move forward not with feelings, but with actions and intentions. You must set your intentions on what you want and then follow with the appropriate actions. You must choose carefully, working not from just feelings but using your head. The choices you make today will affect your tomorrow, so they are very important. You must rise above your feelings when making decisions because your choices cannot be taken lightly.

You may have heard the saying, "You made your bed, now you must sleep in it." It's true. So be mindful and careful of what you choose. Your choices become your story—"the bed you must sleep in." As you create your life, trust that everything is here to teach you and support you on your journey. What you may consider the worst thing ever could potentially turn out to be the best course of events for your growth and transformation. Remain open-minded so that you can see the miracles in every situation. Remember, as human beings, we have a limited vision; we don't always see the whole picture. In fact, it is almost as if we have blinders on. There is always a bigger picture, which may be revealed to us with time if we are open to seeing it. That's where your patience and trust have to come into play. There are always great things ahead if you believe enough to take action regardless of your momentary feelings.

As you peel away the old layers of your life, you get to evolve into a better version of yourself.

Growth is a beautiful gift that never ends until we die, and death itself may actually be a new beginning we know nothing about right now. But growth is not easy. It can be extremely uncomfortable to look at your own weaknesses and actions that you think were wrong—in other words, mistakes. But you are here to be vulnerable and open to change those weaknesses into strengths; there are *no* mistakes. This is a powerful place to stand, to be vulnerable yet strong, to move forward by acknowledging your feelings but still taking action to move forward in your life. You are where you are now to transform yourself into the greatest version you can be, learning to create more light, peace, and love from within so that you can shine brighter inside and outside.

You must not be defined by your feelings for they are not who you are; you can observe and notice them, but do not live your life entirely through them. Take a deep breath and keep moving forward as you learn to get out of your own way, by not getting stuck in your old patterns or old way of being based on your feelings about them. You can be your own worst enemy if you live in your past feelings.

Learning to shift, flow, and move forward even when you don't feel like it or don't know how it will make a difference will help you re-create your life. One foot in front of the other—just keep moving forward. The solution will always be in front of you, not behind you, and the universe/God will support you on this journey.

Don't define yourself by
your circumstances, but rather
by your opportunities.

13. Mindful Choices

Your life is happening exactly how it is
supposed to. Your job is to shift and change.

I cannot stress enough that the choices you make today create what you will experience tomorrow. The choices you make going forward cannot be taken lightly, for they will have a rippling effect in your future. Everything you are and have today is the result of the choices you made at various times in your life. It is not about beating yourself up about the past, but rather it is about figuring out how you want to move forward now.

Trust that whatever you may see as a mistake or challenge supports your future choices and your continued growth. The key is not to get stuck in the past stories but to see them as lessons that strengthen you and your ability to get you closer to what you want. Set a goal to constantly commit to your future growth and development. As you eliminate the things that no longer work and break old habits, you get closer to creating an abundant life.

Learn to make mindful choices today to create a world and a life you love tomorrow. For example, choosing to eat healthy food and getting regular exercise keeps you in shape and healthy as you age. Choosing to stay out of the sun during the sunniest time of the day protects your skin from the sun damage that causes premature aging. Choosing a good partner and uplifting friends on your life's journey gives you the opportunity to co-create a future filled with light and love as a team. An example of a choice I made during my pregnancy was not to gain more weight than I needed to. I ate healthily and exercised while I was pregnant. As a result of that decision, I felt beautiful during and after my pregnancy and had only about five pounds to lose following the birth of my first child.

Although I had no control over my life as a child, I knew certain things were important to me, like keeping myself in shape, looking my best, and having an amazing future. I started by consciously taking control of all that I could in my life. I realized that my looks, my body, and my health are gifts that I will receive only once, so I made the conscious choice to take care of my well-being so that I could enjoy longevity and vitality. Those mindful choices have paid off, and I am grateful.

Discover for yourself what is important to you, and mindfully make the choices that flow with the future you desire.

IT'S YOUR CHOICE

It's your choice to look either at the light or the chaos. Your time here is limited and the chaos will only distract you from bringing more love and light into the world.

14. True Messengers

*Be grateful! You are always supported, loved,
and guided by the messengers in your life.*

A true messenger is anyone who crosses your path who contributes to your life in a beneficial way, teaches you something new, and opens your mind to possibilities and approaches, you may not have been aware of before. They are here to help make your journey easier by sharing their own life experiences with you, like the way a parent might contribute to the growth of their child in an effort to keep them safe, happy, aware, and fulfilled. You may only cross a particular messenger's path once, but they may share a life-changing experience with you that makes a huge difference in your life and gives you a different perspective of your current situation or how to move closer to the future you desire.

The way to recognize a true messenger is by the amount of positive energy they possess. Their intention should be to help guide you and elevate your experience in life. If their experience resonates with you and their words lift your spirit and soul, you may want to take action on what they have to say. A true messenger has nothing to gain by sharing their experience (no ulterior motive);

they are simply giving you tools that can empower you on your path. One of my messengers was the woman at the hair salon I mentioned in chapter 3 who suggested I find a man who adores me. Her message changed the course of my life and narrowed my focus on what was important in a life partner.

We are all messengers in this world; it is our responsibility to spread our love and knowledge with each other to make each other's journey better. We need each other's guidance and wisdom to win at this game called life. True messengers are here to support you and help you shift your life toward your goals and dreams. You must learn to differentiate between the true messengers who are here to contribute to your life in a positive way and false pretend ones who are only out for their own gains and who do not want the best for you.

I have lived most of my life listening to and being guided by the messages of those whose intention was to positively contribute to my life, and I am grateful beyond words for their guidance and love. All these amazing souls have helped me shift the course of my journey and create the life I have today. I am always in search of true messengers and their guidance. I encourage you to keep yourself open, flexible, and thirsty for growth. Remain open to and aware of the messengers coming into your life and see the gifts they have to share with you. You don't have to know how things will unfold, but you must keep walking toward what you want to create.

It's also important to see past the glitz and glamor and the distractions in life to avoid getting caught up in a message that distracts you from your best life. As you clear your path of distractions and eliminate what is not working, you become a clearing for your deepest desires and dreams to manifest.

Here are some messages I'd like to share with you. Perhaps they will inspire you, for that is my intention:

1. Elimination is the path for personal transformation and growth. Eliminate from your life anything that is not taking you closer to what you want to create.

2. Take time to get to know yourself—your likes, your dislikes, and your passion. This is possible when you find an inner connection to yourself and to your inner light and love. Self-acceptance will create the love you seek.

3. The magic you want is inside you; it is not in the outside world, which can be a huge distraction to your true path and happiness. Your job is to unwrap your inner gifts and unique talents and share them with the world. The key is to go deep into yourself and peel away the surface layers of your life so you can find them. For example, my gift is to give my love to others to empower them on their journey.

4. You are greater than you think, so stop believing in self-created limiting beliefs, stories, and opinions that disguise your greatness and sabotage your hopes and dreams.

5. Never give up on yourself. You have a unique gift to contribute to others and the planet. Be a messenger who spreads love and truth to those you encounter. The power is in sharing information with one another.

15. Creating an Easy Childbirth Experience

Anything is possible when you believe in yourself and in your possibility.

Childbirth can be scary for most first-time moms and for pregnant women who had past childbirth experiences that were unpleasant. We've all heard lots of horror stories about childbirth. For first timers, the unknown can be quite frightening and hearing these stories can frighten them further. When I was pregnant with my first child, although I was extremely grateful for this experience, I was also scared. I was searching for answers, seeking comfort, and wanting to learn more about this beautiful time in my life. I, too, had heard many scary stories, but what I wanted was inspiration and comfort, and I found it.

I was a hairdresser at that time, and the hairdresser who worked alongside me had recently become a new mom. So, of course, I asked her questions about childbirth. I immediately recognized her as a true messenger because what she said changed my thinking forever. She said, "Noah, giving birth is fun. I went to the hospital early and received my dose of epidural. My lower body was numb, and I felt nothing. I was smiling, laughing, doing my nails, happy as can be, and when the time came, I pushed that baby out. I felt no pain."

Wow, her story excited me! I decided that this would be my story. I would not listen to anyone who had horror stories about childbirth. My childbirth would be easy and fun, too. I ate healthy food during my pregnancy and exercised regularly to make sure I stayed fit. I took complete charge of creating my experience, and the universe/God supported me. I loved being pregnant, and I felt feminine and beautiful throughout the nine months. I only gained the weight I needed to support my pregnancy. I was able to tell the doctor to massage the baby out so that I wouldn't need an episiotomy. I felt absolutely nothing because I had received the epidural early like I had planned by arriving at the hospital as soon as I thought I was in labor and requested it immediately. I loved giving birth.

My recovery went smoothly, and after the baby weight, water, and placenta were gone, I only had five pounds to lose. Within two weeks, I had a flat belly and I was back to wearing my regular clothes. I duplicated this experience for my other two children. I knew that this was the manifestation of my thoughts and beliefs. I also breastfed all three of my children, an experience I truly loved. Pregnancy, childbirth, breastfeeding, and caring for my babies were priceless and empowering. I am forever grateful for the message I received that day that gave me a belief I chose to make my reality.

What is important here is for you to realize that you do have the power to create your own experiences, to release the ones that cause you discomfort and negative feelings, and connect to the messages that give you faith, peace, and love. You must create your own experiences through positive thinking and self-determination.

When you hold your vision and
take steps toward your desired outcome,
you can manifest your dream. All that
you want is waiting to be discovered.

16. Being a Better Parent

As we help others grow and become free,
we are actually growing and freeing ourselves.
We are all mirrors. Your light is my light.

I've always been hungry for growth and transformation—to be a better mother, a better wife, a better friend, and a better human. I have taken courses, such as Landmark Education (a training and development course), that have helped me on this path, but I have learned that I need to look deeply into my darkest places to really evolve. What I discovered is that my weaknesses can be someone else's strengths, and with their support, I could become stronger.

One of my biggest struggles was learning to manage my family and my children as they got older. Their needs, wants, arguments, and disagreements were difficult to deal with and sometimes overwhelming. For me, parenting has been my biggest challenge, my hardest job. I thought that being a loving mom meant that pleasing my kids was my most important task. I did everything for them, but I was not teaching them how to do things for themselves. I started feeling unappreciated. I had not set clear boundaries for my kids, so our home became a virtual free-for-all. I would get angry and sometimes say hurtful things. I wanted to break that cycle, but I just did not know how.

I really do have sweet, kind, and amazing kids. I knew the problem had to do more with me and my parenting than with them. Our kids are a reflection of us, a perfect mirror of our lives. Whatever we see in them that we do not like is usually within us. We must be patient, set clear boundaries, and be responsible for our own behavior so that they can be responsible for theirs. My strong commitment to take my power back, get answers, and do better as a parent began then and continues through today. I sought and found support, and even hired a wonderful live-in nanny for a month. I made a commitment to not give up on myself, no matter how much I might fall, because I knew that I would learn from my past and do better in my future.

What I realized is that my job as a parent is to be a good teacher because kids are like sponges and copy what they see their parents do. I had to learn to stop controlling what they did and teach them by example. When we stop trying to control the outside world and the people in it, we can become the teachers others may choose to follow. When it comes to creating a better future for our children, we are all responsible for being the best teachers we can be. That's why the self-work is so important.

Creating the life you love is all about growth and never giving up on yourself. In this case, I wanted to create a harmonious family. I did not expect my children, their interactions, or our family life to be perfect. As long as I am alive, my work is not done, and I am always looking for ways to improve and grow.

You, too, are here to grow, transform, and evolve daily, so don't expect perfection ever. There is no such thing as failure or mistakes, only growth. When one way is not working, there is always another path to take that is better for you. The power is in listening to the messages and the messengers. In my case, my children were the messengers I needed to pay attention to. They were mirroring back at me what I needed to do differently. When you listen to the messages you are receiving, you are able to take steps toward a happier and more fulfilling life, the way I did with recognizing what wasn't working in my family.

Like me, I encourage you not to take everything so seriously or make a big deal of every little thing that is happening in your life. Sometimes we get so focused on things that will not matter a month from now. Knowing this, I always look at life from the end perspective. Reviewing my life as if I were on my deathbed, I ask myself, "What do I really care about?" The answer is always the same: my family, my friends, my connections. This always reminds me to not give away my peace to daily nonsense, and this makes me what I want to be: a better parent, a better wife, a better friend, and a better human being.

Remember always the end result of what you are looking to create in your life. For example, if you want a better relationship with your kids, what is it you need to give up today to have that? Stop doing the same thing expecting a different outcome. Our change will create a change in others. We must learn how to get in other people's world and understand their likes and dislikes and their needs. Change cannot occur when we are victims and are only concerned with ourselves.

WHY DO WE GIVE AWAY OUR PEACE?

We are so conditioned to believe that what is important can be found outside us and our relationships. We become fixated on the little annoyances that don't really matter, and we fill our lives with material things that are fleeting. We see what others are doing, and we compete with them to do it better. All of this takes away our peace. If we wait until the end of our lives to recognize what is most important, we may realize that we have given away our peace again and again, and neglected ourselves and our relationships.

At any time, you can make the choice to eliminate any belief that might suggest that having things and getting ahead are more important than nurturing the people and relationships in your life. You can let go of the daily annoyances or triggers that get in the way of experiencing peace in the moment. Having beautiful things and enjoying them are a gift, as long as you don't let them become who you are. Focus instead on the people and connections that can fill your heart and truly make you happy.

17. There Are No Mistakes

Every problem has a solution
if we are open to that possibility.
We are always supported and loved.

We may not understand why things are happening as they are because, as I've mentioned previously, our vision as human beings is limited. We may not be able to see the whole picture as it is right now, just a part of it. Allow me to remind you again to trust that everything is here to support you and teach you to rise above your circumstances and to be powerful in your life. You have total control over yourself and how you react when you are faced with challenges in your life.

To me, the word "mistake" has a negative connotation. Saying that you've made a mistake can make you feel bad and/or wrong—and this feeling can last for a very long time. In fact, it can keep you stuck in the past, not allowing you to move forward in your life today. Telling yourself that you've made a mistake makes you a victim of your past choices and circumstances.

Let's say you just won the lottery. Would you consider

that a mistake? Of course not—it is meant to be yours. You were born, right? You were the fastest sperm. No mistakes! Let's say you learned a hard lesson. Was that a mistake? No! Even the most expensive lessons can shape your future, giving you valuable insight from which you are able to grow and do better moving forward. The key is to look deeper than the surface to see the miraculous lesson in every experience.

Let me give you some examples: A lack of money teaches you to be more responsible and creative in your life to make more money. A bad relationship can teach you about self-love and how to choose better next time. A bad haircut teaches you not to be so attached to your appearance and to have more compassion for yourself. Being sick teaches you to be grateful for your health and how to take better care of yourself.

You are exactly where you need to be at every minute and what you consider mistakes are just a part of your own evolution and growth. You are here on a journey of growth and transformation. Therefore, keep rising to your greatest self. Everything is an opportunity for you to shed what doesn't work, evolve, and transform. Of course not every transformation comes without heartache, pain, or grief. Sometimes the lessons are big, and sometimes the lessons are small, but the truth remains that you are always learning lessons. Your lessons on your journey take you exactly where you need to go so that you can learn exactly what you need to learn.

Once you have been able to shed what no longer serves your life and let go of the idea that the mistakes you think you've made are holding you back, everything will come to you at the perfect time, as I've mentioned previously. It is simply a matter of making your choices and living with those choices until you have an opportunity to make better choices. When you disconnect from what is not empowering you, you are able to discover what inspires you.

Avoid letting yourself be defined by other people's opinions of the choices you've made. Their belief systems and opinions do not define you! Love yourself unconditionally. Find others who love you and believe in you, even when you can't do it yourself. Being grateful for the lessons and opportunities available to you in every situation is key to your constant growth toward change. When you learn to trust the process and your own evolution on this journey, knowing that the solutions are always in front of you, you will then hold the key to your happiness, love, and peace.

When you take the inner journey into yourself and let go of any perceived faults or mistakes, you will find that the light inside you is strong and always wanting to guide you. This takes consciously going inward every day and turning on your light before you step into the outside world. By doing that you can find your center and peace. You can do this in many different ways. Some examples include yoga, journaling, drawing, meditation, being kind to yourself, and keeping a gratitude journal.

Stop beating yourself up for things you think you did not do correctly because they no longer matter; you are an amazing light that simply needs constant connection and love. Regardless of what you think of your past, walk with your head up high every day, knowing that you are the light that shines from within. Find your mind, body, and soul connection, and fall in love with you. Don't define yourself by your past challenges. Separate yourself from what has happened to you and what you made that mean. You are not your challenges, you are not your past, and you are not the stories you tell yourself. Remember that there are no mistakes, only lessons that support you in your growth.

The only thing you are responsible for is how you show up every day in your life going forward. Mindfully and consciously make choices to bring into your life things that empower you on your journey, things that lift your spirit and soul. Live in the present moment, and let go of what was, and be grateful for what is right now.

The flow of gratitude impacts our attitude.
Today, be grateful for you are, who you
are becoming, and who you will be.

18. Less Judgment, More Compassion

Everything we are is mirrored in our world; we must have more compassion and less judgment for ourselves so that we can have it for others.

As humans, we naturally judge everything. We judge ourselves, our environment, and each other. It's a natural human emotion. There is a lot of benefit to judging things: It keeps us more aware, safe, and present to our surroundings. But judgments also create divisions among us and bring negative energy into our lives. We see others as less capable, sometimes stupid, or less than us. We make them wrong for what we perceive as their mistakes, even though we sometimes make unwise choices ourselves. Our judgments stop us from truly forgiving others and ourselves for their humanity and ours.

No one is perfect. We are all humans, and to err is human. When you judge others, you lose your compassion and love for them. The same is true when you judge yourself. Always remember that you are not your troubles, your worries, your weaknesses, or your thoughts. You must learn to separate any poor choices you may have made from who you truly are, and the same is true of others. When you can start replacing your self-judgment with love and compassion, you will naturally start replacing judgment of others with love and compassion. Your non-judgment of others helps elevate them and navigate their obstacles. Compassion for others is directly connected to compassion for yourself.

We all need forgiveness, love, and compassion, yet they seem so hard to give, especially to those closest to us who need them the most. So begin by letting go of judgments of those people who are closest to you. As you release your judgments of them, you are also releasing your own self-judgments. You are freeing yourself from your own bondage, limiting ideas, thoughts, and patterns that have become your reality and your obstacles over time. When you send compassion to others, you are sending it to yourself as well. Again, it is the mirror of each other. You think you are helping another, yet in truth, you are really helping yourself. This is because, as I've mentioned, we are all one.

Your judgments create a prison of sorts in which you are a prisoner without even realizing it. The prison is devoid of love and compassion, making the world feel heavy, negative, and dark at times. To release yourself, let go of the limited beliefs and opinions that are locking you in you. It is not easy to unlearn everything you know, but it is a chance to be better, do better, care more, and love more deeply. When you are free, you have the opportunity to evolve into a greater version of yourself and be happier, peaceful, free, and self-expressed more in the world.

TEACH YOUR CHILDREN

When you practice non-judgment in your life, you create love and compassion for yourself. You are then in the amazing position to teach future generations the path of compassion and love. I live by these words: "Treat people the way you want to be treated." Teach your children to practice non-judgment with themselves, so that they can learn to treat others with compassion and love, and then teach their own children this same lesson. In this way, future generations will lead a better life with an open heart. Making an impact on the next generation is the most important thing any of us can do for the future of this planet. We all need each other, and together we *can* change the world for the better and live a happier life.

19. The Power of Forgiveness

When we let go of our old stories, resentments,
fears, and anger, we are left only with love.

One of the most important things you can do is find forgiveness for yourself and others. Forgiveness frees you from the chains that keep you stuck in life and gives you the freedom to create something new. You let go of past resentment and anger and live a more happy and peaceful life as a result.

You may find forgiveness a very difficult thing to do for so many reasons. You might think that if you forgive others, you are making what they have done okay or giving them a free pass. However, forgiveness is simply releasing yourself from your past and giving yourself the freedom to be more expressive in the world. It does not matter who is right or who is wrong; what matters is that you no longer hold on to the past resentments, anger, and fear that you once did. When you put out anger, fear, and resentment, you live in anger, fear, and resentment. When you put out love and light, you live in love and light. This is the magic of forgiveness, even if you don't see it right now.

Forgiveness melts all negativity and creates the harmony we seek within ourselves and the outside world.

Forgiveness is a huge part of my life always. I learned over time how much the past resentments and fears were keeping me from moving forward and living a self-expressed life. What I realized is that when I let go of old stories, resentments, fears, and anger, I was left only with love and compassion. I am a firm believer that we all win when we help each other, and this includes helping each other heal and rise above our past conflict. When you truly forgive, you give yourself and the other person permission to heal and move forward in life. You don't have to have them in your life, but you can still send them your forgiveness, love, and light. Each one of us wants forgiveness and the chance to move forward in our lives. So why not help each other?

I have a beautiful story to share with you about forgiveness. On this journey, I was blessed to meet Denise through an online ad. My coach advised me to hire someone to help me with my kids and errands because I always seemed to be running around a lot. Denise answered the ad immediately, and our connection was instant. I knew she was the perfect person to help me. However, I had no idea that what I needed her for was different from what I had hired her to do initially. I truly believe there are no mistakes; Denise and I were meant to cross each other's paths.

One day, while I was working on my book, which was going slowly because I am not a fast typist, I asked Denise if she was a fast typist. She said yes. Talk about the universe/God bringing the perfect person into my life! I was beyond grateful. Denise and I spent a lot of time together, at least three days a week. I dictated my book to her and her fingers flew over the keyboard. She also helped me with two other important tasks: taking my kids to school and taking my dog, Snowy, to the dog park. Over time, Denise and I got to know each other and realized we had similar pasts. As we were working together, Denise was telling me how much my book spoke to her and how she related to so much of it. I felt like my book was helping her heal, and she did also. In that moment, I knew that my book would help others heal and strengthen their lives.

Denise had been going through her own challenges and growth, just like we all do. This was a big year for her; a lot of changes were happening in her life. While many of them were great changes, any kind of change takes adjustment and time before it becomes a comfortable part of our lives. A main thing Denise was dealing with at the time was that she had not spoken to her family for a long time. Past traumas, resentments, and anguish had caused a huge gap in time. To be more exact, it had been twenty-two years since she had spoken to her mom.

One day, she received an unexpected telephone call from a cousin she had not heard from in years, telling her that her mom was dying of cancer and was in hospice care. The family wanted to let her know and felt that Denise should call her mother. Her first reaction was "There's no way in hell I am calling her!" She remembered how she had always believed she would have a conversation with her mother on her deathbed and ask whether she was aware of certain abuses Denise had suffered as a child.

Denise spoke with several friends over the weekend about her mother. She asked me my opinion, and this is what I told her: "Call your mom and just tell her that you love her. You can come from love and light and forgiveness and make peace with her and give yourself peace. You can give her a peaceful transition, as well as set yourself free."

When Denise heard those words, "You can give her a peaceful transition," she was overcome with emotion, and she knew she could and had to give that to her mother.

She spent the weekend soul searching and found the love that was always in her heart for her mother. She wanted to forgive her mom, and decided she had to find peace for both of them before it was too late. Denise gathered her thoughts and, pulling from every ounce of strength in her being, she picked up the telephone and called her mom on Sunday morning. Her stepfather would not allow her to speak with her mother. She called twice more, and no one answered the phone.

Denise decided to leave her mother a message. This is what she said: "Hi Mom. It's Denise. I'm sorry and I forgive you for everything. I would like for us both to be at peace. I'm sorry we could not have made peace sooner. Tell Grandma and Grandpa I love and miss them, and I will love and miss you, too. Please call me if you would like to talk. Good-bye, Mom. I love you."

Denise did not believe she would hear from her mother, but felt a love, a peace, and a calm she had not known for her mother in a very long time.

Sunday evening Denise received a call from her brother, whom she had also not spoken with in about seven years. She could not believe she was speaking to her brother! He said the family had heard her message. He explained that their mom was in and out of consciousness and in a lot of pain, but her brother said her sister was sharing Denise's message with their mom whenever she was lucid. Denise was filled with gratitude that her mother would hear her words. She asked her brother if they could be friends again, and he said yes. He went on to tell Denise that their mother had approximately ten days to live. Denise hung up the phone, devastated over the news but overjoyed to be part of her brother's life again. She was full of love and forgiveness for her whole family now.

Denise woke up Monday morning with feelings full of regret for the many wasted years, and decided to go see her mother. Within hours, she was on the next flight. When she walked into her mother's room, she found a frail, devastatingly thin shell of the mother she once had so many hurt feelings for. Now she looked at her and felt only love, forgiveness, and compassion.

Her mother was heavily drugged due to the enormous amount of pain she was in. Even after twenty-two years coupled with the drugs and pain of the cancer eating away at her body, Denise's mother knew her instantly. They shared a connection of pure love they had never known before. They shared life stories and only spoke of the love and affection they always had for each other. They also agreed that they were both stubborn women, but that it also made them strong women. Denise showed her mom pictures of her grandsons, one she had not seen since the age of two and one she never knew.

Denise looks very much like her mother, and it occurred to her then and she told her mom, "I look just like you, so I have seen you every day."

Denise's mom passed away peacefully, surrounded by all three of her children and her husband. Today Denise has her family back in her life. They enjoy holidays together and are always there for each other. This is the power of forgiveness: to find connection to yourself and the people you love most; to release anger and resentment and live a happy and fulfilled life.

This story of forgiveness is one of the most beautiful I have ever heard.

***Our commitment to love and compassion
will transform our relationships and
shift our lives toward wholeness.***

20. **Taking Responsibility for You**

Life is multilayered. The question is,
which layer do you choose to live in?

You have no control over what other people do or say. The only person you have control over is yourself. Learn to take responsibility for everything—the good, the bad, the challenging, the beautiful, and the ugly. This is definitely an extremely challenging and difficult task for all of us. It takes a lot of courage with a new mindset to execute. It does not come to most of us naturally. It is part of your own awakening and bringing more consciousness to your life. You are no longer at the mercy of others and what they do, but rather, you are the creator of your life.

When you think of taking responsibility, it may at first feel uncomfortable and heavy. You live in a world where most people would rather blame each other than be accountable when things go wrong. It's a learned limiting behavior that it is important to change in order to live a powerful life. We see it in our families, in our schools, and at our jobs. I always tell my children when you point a finger at someone else, there are three fingers pointing at you. How do you learn to give up the blame? You must realize there is a cost for your blame that you are paying, and you are not giving it up for nothing. You see, when you choose to give up blaming others for what is not working in your life, you actually gain a gift you give yourself. You become more powerful.

Taking responsibility lets you look deeper into any situation, instead of just seeing what is happening on the surface. You take a step back like a spectator observing your own life. *What can I learn here? How can I shift because the blame game is not giving me a life I love? Why am I repeating old cycles and not living the life that I want? Why am I attracting situations where I feel powerless in my life?* Taking responsibility gives you an opportunity to shift your consciousness, your life, and allows you to grow. You start realizing your impact on the world and others. You stop trying to change others and work on your own growth and development.

When you take responsibility for what is not working right now, you can also take credit for what you are creating at every moment by being powerful and responsible. It's all in your control, and you get to say how you would like to move forward today. You learn to take appropriate actions that help you grow into the best version of you and inspire you to do your best daily.

The Cost of Blame	The Payoff for Responsibility
You give away your power to others.	You get to be powerful in your life.
You feel like a victim, controlled by others.	You get to have control over your own life and future.
You have no emotional control.	You are grounded and open to receive abundance.
You feel out of control.	You are conscious of your behavior and your impact on others.
You are confused and directionless.	You have clarity and a clear path to your destiny.

ELIMINATION

Elimination is the first step in taking responsibility for yourself. It is the key to your success. As you eliminate things that are keeping you from totally expressing yourself in the world, you create new paths and openings to create a life you love.

Elimination is the key to creating your most perfect life. The more you eliminate the things that don't work for you, the faster you create the things that will work and flow easily in your life.

How do you start to eliminate roadblocks that prevent your gratitude and growth? Saying no is one way. Start to say no to those things that will come between you and your happiness. This could be as small as making sure you are true to the time you have dedicated to yourself. If you create those thirty minutes a day for yourself, stick to it! Don't let others pressure you into denying yourself that time.

Evaluate what and where you are putting your energy into and begin to assess how much you really need to dedicate to those things. Be intentional with your time, and always have a purpose and goal that you can move toward.

Try journaling! There is so much power in writing down your mission and goals. Writing your dreams down with pen and paper is the first step of actually accomplishing what you want to achieve. Eliminate anything from your life that isn't in alignment with your mission and goals and what you are committed to creating in your life. It's your responsibility to make it happen.

21. The Gift of Rejection

Be grateful for the people who
contribute to you and help lift your soul.
Be grateful for those who don't,
for they are teaching you self-love.

When you start realizing that the rejections you experience in life are here to support you rather than hurt you, you are more open to receive what is meant for you. I lived much of my life guided by rejection. If I honored the rejection, it always guided me toward a better path. However, if I remained attached to a certain outcome, even though I'd been rejected, it would wind up not being the right path or direction in my life.

Why is it that rejection is so hard for us to accept? Why is it that sometimes we are so stubborn, we wind up only hurting ourselves in the end? Rejection's job is to guide you toward the right path, yet you may see it as your biggest enemy and the source of your pain and suffering.

In my own life, time and time again, I noticed that when I went against my guided path and did not listen to the message in the rejection, I was always taking the more difficult path. And that's okay, too, since sometimes you need to grow and learn for yourself so you can see more clearly in the future. You must realize that this journey is supported and guided, and everything is the way it is for a reason, even if it does not make sense to you right now.

The greatest lesson you can learn is to be a good listener because the signs are always there to guide you to your most abundant life. Your job is to trust the guidance of the universe/God and have faith that there is always a bigger plan you may not be able to see or understand now. This is not an easy thing to do, but it is definitely the path of least resistance. Taking the path of least resistance means living a life that flows toward peace and happiness in the long run. The little battles in life come and go, like they were never there, but winning the war is the gift and your victory over your past.

The war of wanting to be accepted and loved by others is going on within ourselves. However, you should be unwilling to sacrifice your own well-being, peace, and happiness in the process. That is why the rejection you experience is so important. Without it, you cannot keep moving toward the life you truly want and desire.

Rejection and elimination have a lot in common. They both guide you toward all that you desire. The only difference is that rejection is you being guided by others, and it may not feel great at the time. We tend to take rejection personally, as if it means that we are not worthy or good enough, which is totally not true. All it means is that it is time to move forward and create a new path that can enrich your life even more. When you let go of attachment to how things should be and embrace how they are unfolding, you are free to step in the right direction.

There is always a bigger picture, which will eventually be revealed to you at the perfect time. Everything people do to you is a reflection of them, not a reflection of you. The rejection you experience is your guide, not your enemy; it wants you to move forward toward a better life and future.

Elimination is taking the power of rejection into your own hands. It means your self-confidence is strong and you are at a place in your life where you know what you want and need. You start realizing the power that is inside you, and you know you can create anything you want when you believe in yourself and your life. You are ready to co-create with the universe/God that which you know you deserve. You are focused on your goals and are open to receive all the great gifts and miracles the world has to offer you. Your faith and trust are bigger than your fears, and you know it is up to you to create a life you love. You are moving forward with intention and purpose, knowing that you are the creator of your future life. You get to choose who comes into your life, and you don't settle for less than what you know you deserve. You realize that you have the power of choice and know that you are responsible for your own well-being and happiness always.

When you truly understand the power of rejection and elimination, you can welcome them into your life with more acceptance and love. It is just part of your growth and transformation to learn to connect to, instead of rejecting, the very things that are here to help guide you to a better tomorrow.

As always, learning to get out of your own way and being kind to yourself is most important. It is also important to connect to others who have total appreciation and love for who you are on the inside, not just on the outside. The kinder you are to yourself, the more kindness you will expect from others in your life. It is all in your hands to be a seeker in this life and not settle for less than you deserve. You must see your own greatness and love yourself so much that anything less than what you deserve will always be rejected.

It really comes down to knowing how to listen and having high expectations of yourself and others. Listen to others to see if they are in alignment with your path and what you want. If not, wish them the best and keep moving forward on your journey. Never sacrifice who you are to fit into other people's standards. Hold yourself to a high standard and let them meet you where you are. The wrong people and connections will fall by the wayside, while the right ones will continue to grow and help you fly.

The universe/God is always communicating with you and guiding you. The question is: Are you listening to its messages?

22. Your Lowest Lows Can Lead You to Your Highest Highs

*Every uphill climb has a downward slope,
and every low has a high; one cannot exist
without the other. Meet yourself exactly
where you are with love and compassion.*

Your challenges should not define you. You must learn to separate them from who you are. When you associate your challenges with who you are, you are likely to disconnect from and resent yourself.

Always remember: You are not your past! You are not your challenges! You are not your stories! You are a light, the energy force, that shines inside and outward into the world daily. When you are able to start forgiving yourself, you will find peace deep within your heart and soul. No matter what you are going through, remember that everything in life is temporary. Trust in a higher power—the universe, God, whatever you believe in—to get you through any situation. Meet yourself exactly where you are at this time with love, forgiveness, and compassion, always. This will lead you to new heights.

Miracles are happening at all times, everywhere, and there is usually a solution to every situation and problem. An ending is only the beginning of a new journey and path. You have the power to move forward out of any situation or make the best of your circumstances right now. You are not broken; you are just disconnected and need to realign with yourself and what you truly desire in this lifetime.

Be aware that reconnecting to yourself can bring up a lot of discomfort. You start seeing how your actions have affected your life and the lives of others around you. You are being awakened to a new consciousness and awareness. That wakefulness will make you more present in your life now. This awareness causes you to see yourself more clearly, which may cause you to be judgmental and resentful toward yourself. That's why self-acceptance, forgiveness, and compassion are so important. They help you love yourself, no matter what you are feeling and no matter what others say or do. Remember, you can only be responsible for yourself.

When you trust in the universe/God, there will be a light at the end of every tunnel. To see the light, let go of a victim mentality and know that whatever you have created in your life can be re-created the way you want it to be. This takes a strong self-commitment to breaking old cycles or behaviors and creating a new structure to build your life upon now.

To grow, you need to constantly create new, more empowering cycles in your life. Although growth may be painful, everything is here to teach you a lesson so that you can move forward with more power and intention. You have the power to move forward when you have learned the lessons from your past.

A great example of that is the romantic partner you choose in your life. Sometimes you keep choosing the wrong partner, one who does not treat you well or help you grow. It's an old pattern or cycle that keeps repeating itself in your life. Once you get awakened to your choices, you can make better choices in your future. Beating yourself up for your past decisions does not create forward movement or growth in your life. It just keeps you a victim in your life today.

The key is to notice, awaken, and create a new commitment to yourself right now. Take the opportunity to learn, grow, and re-create what you really want. This is part of peeling back the layers of your life to get closer to your true self and your innermost desires. Remember, there is nothing wrong; there is just what is happening now. This is a chance for you to rise higher than ever before.

Every uphill has a downhill, and vice versa, just like life. It's how you deal with those challenges that shapes who you are. Take time to be with yourself and stop trying to find answers in others. You have the power and knowledge to raise your life to new levels.

Take the time to make a plan and write down the things you most want, then make an action plan with steps to move you forward toward your dreams. Action plus intention equals the life you love. It's up to you to uncover the peace, love, and joy you desire.

There is always support out there when you are open to receive it. You can find great messengers, therapists, courses, books, and friends who will be happy to lend support when you are ready and willing to be open to receive them. The first step is to realize that you are ready for a change now, knowing that you may have to give up certain things in your life that are holding you back in the present moment. Anything you want to change is possible when you are ready and have faith and trust in yourself and your journey. Allow your lowest lows to elevate your life by letting them go and rising above them.

> **You are not your past.**
> **You are not your stories.**
> **You are not your judgments.**
> **You are not what you own.**
> **You are not what you do.**
> **You are not your problems.**
> **You are the light that shines in the world.**
> **Connect to your light and shine.**

23. The Flow of Gratitude

Be grateful for what is working and for what is not.
Everything is here to help you shift and change.

When things are working, they flow easily from space to space. You don't need to fight for them too hard. The same goes for your friendships and relationships. Life is ever-changing and flowing forward, minute by minute, hour by hour, and day by day. Nothing stays the same. It is so important to be grateful for what's happening right now and appreciate this chance to live and grow daily.

Earlier I talked about allowing yourself to flow like water, effortlessly through life. This is possible when you let go of anything that holds you back and connect to your love and light through the power of gratitude. You would no longer be fighting or resisting, but rather moving through life more easily, fluidly, and powerfully forward. Everything flows forward, and so must you.

The most powerful way to create flow in life is to be connected to gratitude. Gratitude flows just like life; it keeps you present to your appreciation and love. It keeps you focused on the miracles that surround you daily. Your gratitude keeps you connected and happy and keeps your internal energy moving as well as your external energy. The movement of your energy creates a perfect balance of mind, body, and soul connection.

When we have gratitude for this journey and trust in the universe/God as well as ourselves, we realize that everything happens for a bigger reason. As I've mentioned previously, you may not understand why things happen because you can't always see the full picture. That's where trust and faith come in. You must believe the universe/God wants the best for you, even when it may not seem so right now. You must overcome your own limited beliefs in order to rise to your highest self. You are here to evolve and win, not to suffer.

When you realize that you are supported and loved in this life, you can give yourself permission to let go, flow, and trust, being grateful for your experiences in every moment. There are always things in your life that may be out of balance or order. It's important to find gratitude for these situations, too, because they are teaching you something and giving you the opportunity to grow and change.

I look at life as a collage. Each person's collage is sprinkled with dots of varying sizes. The little dots represent replaceable things, even though their loss may cause us some discomfort. The bigger dots represent things that are close to our heart, irreplaceable things like health, our family, our loved ones, and ourselves. Those are the things worth living for; they are the roots of our life. Focus your gratitude on your "big dots" and do not let the "little dots" control your life. Look at your collage and notice the parts of your life that are working perfectly and smoothly; you must focus on that. Focusing on what really matters keeps you centered in gratitude and love, making it easier to flow through and beyond anything that is not working. When you are truly connected to your flow of gratitude, you learn to be grateful even for those things that are not working. Again, trust that everything happens the way it should, even if it's beyond your understanding at the time. You must always trust and believe that the universe/God wants only the best for you. As you learn to have faith and trust in your journey and believe in yourself, you can see the blessings life has to offer and recognize that what you perceive as obstacles are here to help you climb above them and rise to your greatest self.

When you bring your awareness to all that is working and flowing effortlessly in your life, you become consciously connected to your gratitude and love. Being in connection with what really matters shifts your whole perception into one of gratitude and love, bringing your awareness to your greenest grass. The more you focus on your gratitude, the happier you will be, living your life with purpose and love. A connection to yourself, your life, and your gratitude will fill your heart with love and lift your soul daily.

HOW TO CREATE AN INSPIRED LIFE

I am the power that drives my life;
I can shift and change because I believe in me.

To create an inspired life, begin by becoming grateful for what you do have and what is currently working in your life. Gratitude encourages movement and flow. If your energy isn't flowing forward, how can you grow and move forward in your life? This includes being grateful for the smallest things such as having a place to sleep and live, having food to eat, a body that is functioning and alive, and also having free will and freedom to make choices to evolve, grow, and change.

How can you find more gratitude in your life? Don't get stuck for too long! The process of elimination helps you remove roadblocks that are standing in the way of your flow and gratitude. You must learn to grow connected to them both! Everything has a way around it. Sometimes the road is hard to see, but that doesn't mean it is not there. Letting things go is part of the flow of gratitude.

Eliminate anything that is preventing you from feeling grateful. These things can be both mental and physical. Letting go of toxic relationships and people will also bring you closer to your truth and self-love. Your judgments and opinions can slow you down and prevent you from being more accepting and loving in your life and toward others. Learning to release what no longer serves you is the key to moving forward with gratitude and love.

24. Focus on What Is Working

The solution is always in front of you;
keep moving toward it.

What you focus on really does create your reality. You will always be faced with challenges that can get you stuck within yourself if you focus too much on them. You move in transit all day long from one moment to another. Sometimes that movement seems easy and effortless; other times, it feels heavy and out of your control. You can only control yourself, your mind, your thoughts, and your emotions. You cannot control others and what they do or think.

You may find yourself focusing on the things in your life that are not working, while forgetting all that is working perfectly for you right now. When you focus on what is not working, it brings up stress, resentment, anger, and other negative emotions. When you realize that everything else is working perfectly, you can bring peace and happiness back into your mind and life. As I've said before, the solutions are always in front of you. Sometimes you just have to trust and let go, walk away, breathe, and re-create.

This constantly flexes the muscle of gratitude in your life. Focusing on your gratitude for the seemingly smallest things, like having your health, your eyes, your legs, and so on, can be enough to bring you back to what really counts. This gratitude helps you focus on what is flowing in your life rather than get stuck in the stories about what's going wrong. Keeping in mind that everything is here to teach you and help you grow more into the person you are meant to be in this world will keep you grounded and focused on the solutions.

The solutions are within you, but to get to them, you must learn to listen and be open to receive; this takes focus. Take action to create a solution to the problems you are facing. Don't let the problem become your focus and take over your life. Have compassion for yourself as you move forward and past anything you want to change. There is *always* support out there, but you must seek the answers. Learn to breathe, clear your mind, and get clarity on what you really want to create. Then write it down. When you write things down, they already start manifesting. Ask the universe/God for guidance, and I promise the messenger will come to help you when you are open to receive, always.

Do not let your feelings about a situation control your outcomes. You must use your head, your brain, to make a decision on how to move forward. Decisions that are based purely on feelings, as I mentioned earlier, are usually weak in their foundation. With that said, you also don't want to "be in your head" all day long. It's been said that being in your head is like being in a "bad neighborhood" and it's true, especially when you are so focused on negative emotions you become more unhappy in your life. Take control of your mind, and focus on your gratitude instead. Learn to take the next step forward, not backward. Know that six months from now, much of what is currently happening will be forgotten and gone. If you learn the lessons of your challenges, you will not have to repeat them again. No lesson is too expensive if you learn something from it, and believe me, I have had many expensive lessons, but they are the very things that have helped me transform and grow into who I am today, so I am grateful for them.

Life will seem to flow more effortlessly when you focus on keeping your energy moving forward. You will be happier and more connected to yourself and your life. You will be able to be more responsible for your emotions and how you impact others. Life will become happier, and you will no longer be under the influence of your circumstances. You will become the leader of your life, and you will shine your light on the world and others. You will be full of gratitude and love, able to take those gifts out into the world and help effect a shift in consciousness for all who seek growth and change.

25. Stepping Out of Fear

Fear will freeze you, but love will free you!
We must not let others' fears become our truth.

I lived much of my life in fear and kept myself hidden from the world. My fear became so real that I even made up a story that I kept playing like a movie in my head. That story kept me feeling small and fearful most of my life.

As a child, I loved watching cartoons on Saturday mornings. One morning, I saw an image on the screen that I connected to and adopted as my own. In the cartoon, the kids are waiting for the school bus to pick them up on the first day of school. One of the kids is really scared and nervous to get on the big yellow bus for the first time. As the bus pulls up to him, he shrinks into a tiny dot. The bus is huge, the world is huge, it is scary out there, and therefore, the child in the cartoon feels he is insignificant in the big world.

For most of my life, that story made perfect sense to me. *This is me*, I thought. Fear and insignificance became my story and I adopted that image I saw on the screen.

But I was stronger than I thought. There was a spark of energy and strength always moving through me. That's why I also identified with Wonder Woman; I wanted to be able to turn around and transform into a powerful woman, just like her—and eventually I did.

Fear will never give you the life you want! I always say, "Fear will freeze you, but love will free you." Fear will freeze you until you are able to step into it and trust the journey and that the universe/God has your back. It is up to you to step into your greatest self, to have faith that the universe/God is there to support you in every way. You must take the action toward the life you want. Even one little step forward toward your dreams starts creating them already.

The universe/God wants you to have it all and will support you every step of the way. It is safe to move forward now. This is the perfect time to release your past, your disempowering stories, your limiting beliefs, and your fears and to start freeing yourself to live the life you truly desire. Always remember that you are here to grow and transform into the greatest version of yourself. You must realize you are not your past or your stories. Find ways to let go of your past limiting thoughts and feelings about yourself. Those are some of the things that hold you back the most. Find a support system, a coach, a yoga or meditation class, and others who see your greatness to help guide you on this path and empower you. Support systems are so important to help you see your own greatness.

Being able to separate yourself from how you perceived yourself earlier in life and moving powerfully forward is the key to creating a new story of love and happiness. The past should no longer define you or your life today. When you let go of what was said and done to you and choose to no longer be controlled by that, you will be able to set yourself and your life free by breaking chains that are still keeping you hostage to fear, unworthiness, and self-doubt.

Most of the chains you wear today are limiting beliefs, visions, and opinions that are not empowering you in your life. They are negative fields of energy that you live in without a clear vision of your own potential. These barriers and filters keep you stuck in your own reality, like an old movie, rather than help you move forward to create a new possibility. When you listen to the media, the news, the glitz, the glamour, the opinions of others, TV, radio, internet, ask yourself, "How is this forwarding my mission, my life, my happiness?" Eliminate anything that creates fear or self-doubt in your life for it does not serve your forward flow.

Anything that takes you away from moving forward in life can cause depression, sadness, lack of performance, limited vision, indecisiveness, and feelings of being out of control and frightened. You become stuck and you do not know how to break the cycle. You give away your love, power, happiness, and dreams to things that do not take you where you want to go. You decide that life is too stressful and limited and continue to live as if you are in the movie of your limiting beliefs.

Learning to break any cycles of negativity and fear in your life can only be done with a hunger in your soul to grow and break the cycle you knew in the past. Going inward into yourself is where the magic begins. Finding your inner love, courage, and connection gives your journey a new beginning. Finding time to sit quietly in meditation or just breathing intentionally can make a huge difference in your outlook and perception. Journaling your thoughts and ideas can help you get clear about your likes and dislikes. Yoga is also a great way to connect to yourself with breath and movement; yoga helps you grow from within. Landmark Education or similar courses can empower you to take action.

Surround yourself with like-minded individuals with whom you feel safe, people who empower you, see your greatness, and lift your soul.

Learn to ask the universe/God for help and guidance; they are always willing and open to help you learn and grow. All you have to do is seek and the answers will come to you at the perfect time when you are ready.

Don't give up on yourself and continue to live in fear. Keep playing this game called life, growing and becoming a greater version of yourself by bravely stepping out of your fears.

As you shed the things that keep you feeling fearful, victimized, or insignificant, you are able to replace them with self-confidence, empowerment, love, and joy. You get to step into your light and love every day and feel great about yourself, your life, and your journey. You shine your light on others, allowing them to see their own greatest potential. You are connected to your light and shine from the inside out and make the world a better, safer place for all. You get to write a new story and break the old cycles of fear and scarcity once and for all. You get to enrich and change the lives of future generations.

You do this work for you, for them, for future children, and in return, everybody wins. Your story can become full of magic and miracles that inspire others to continue moving past their own fears by creating empowering stories of their own. Energy feeds on energy. Love feeds on more love. Know that there are miracles to uncover, and as love is brought forward, it will create magic in your life. It is really up to you to take the steps toward whatever you desire. All it takes is getting out of your head and into your faith and trust, one step at a time, and know that you will rise above your fears and succeed if you believe in you.

Have faith and trust in yourself,
and life will support you. You are meant
to grow and rise to your greatest self.

26. Now Is the Perfect Time

You are stronger and more powerful than your circumstances. Change stressful to grateful.

So often we feel like we wish we had made better choices at an earlier time in our lives. We keep looking back into our past, saying, *If only I did that sooner. If only I started that job sooner or found that house sooner or met the perfect mate sooner, things would have been much better. If only I knew then what I know now.*

We can be really hard on ourselves. Somehow, we are constantly wanting to bring our past into our present and future. It's time to realize that the past will never be again and be grateful for this present moment because that is all any of us have right now.

It seems that no one gets a free pass. You have probably had many challenges along your journey. As I have been discussing, those challenges are the very things that get you to look deeper into your life and desire more for yourself. You are always the student of life, here to learn, evolve, and grow with time. Your insights, your growth, and your development happen at the perfect time, when you are ready for it. You are not born walking, but through the process of growth and development, you get there.

There is a time for everything. The universe/God has a divine time for when everything happens. Your development happens when you are ready and open to receive guidance, and then everything is ready to open and reveal itself to you. It's the process of uncovering your true gifts so you can enjoy them along the way. You cannot move forward powerfully without the right tools in hand and without the lessons along the way. All you have is this present time to appreciate all you have accomplished and be grateful for this moment in your life.

I see life as a staircase that with every step, a new challenge or opportunity gets me closer to my goal. I take small steps upward and know that I will get there in the right time, one rung at a time. I am excited for my growth, and I know today is just a new day in a lifetime of creation. I trust that the universe/God wants me to keep moving forward in my life, and they have unseen intelligence and know the time when things need to open, bloom, ripen.

You are blooming minute by minute, day by day, and season by season. Just look back and see how far you have come. There is no need to compare where you are to anyone else; you can be peaceful, knowing you are supported and loved always. Put energy into things that ignite your passion. When you do what you love, you bring abundance to your own life and the world.

Fifteen years ago, I said I was going to write this book, yet it was sitting in my head all this time. I was not ready. I had to do my own growth to come to a place where I could share my message and my story with you. You cannot beat yourself up for your past, and you must realize creation happens right now, in this present moment. All that is guaranteed to you is this moment.

Can you learn to pause and see the magic in right now? Can you look at the people you love with utmost compassion and love, especially you? Can you be present to how they contribute to you in your life every day? Bring awareness to all the gifts you are given and how far you have come. This moment is priceless. This is your journey. Keep moving forward while being grateful for the now because *now* is the perfect time.

NOT ENOUGH TIME?

Focus, commitment, intentionality, and action
are all aligning as we create a life we love.

There is always enough time to do what you need to get done. The question is not how much time do you have, but how are you using that time? Are you being intentional with your time, or are you getting caught up doing mindless things and not being aware of the passage of time? You must learn to prioritize and structure the things that are essential for forward movement.

For example, it was really important to me to finish my book to get my message out in the world and help others, yet so many days I would not write. I would get stuck on the small stuff that took me out of my own creation and flow. If something is important, you need to act like it is and keep focused on it by being intentional. Don't let people, media, Facebook, Instagram, TV, games, or any other distractions get in the way of moving forward in your life. Those habits can keep you stuck in your head and stagnant.

You must learn that what you want to create cannot happen until you set an intention to make those things the most important part of your daily life. To write my book, I had to make it a number-one priority in the now. Other things had to take a backseat. The first thing I did once my kids went to school in the morning was sit down and write. I knew that was the only way my book would get finished, without letting anything get in my way.

As you build new habits by setting priorities and eliminating distractions, you shift your life, thereby creating more time to try out new opportunities and elevate your path.

27. Getting Comfortable with Being Uncomfortable

To get comfortable, it is necessary to get uncomfortable by stepping into our fears, shifting, and creating change.

Part of growing up and evolving comes from your willingness to get uncomfortable at times so that you can learn and grow from things that might scare you but that support you in taking your next step. Remain open and flexible so that you can receive more of life's gifts. It's a "wax-on-wax-off" action that eventually gets you to your greatness. It's the unseen work and investment in yourself and your life that will eventually pay off.

Immediate gratification in life is not sustainable or lasting. You may not always enjoy the process of moving outside your comfort zone, but you will enjoy the long-term rewards. For example, if you want to share your message with others, but you are afraid of public speaking, find a way to start sharing yourself rather than choosing to stay comfortable in your head. Public speaking classes like Toastmasters can help you. The question is always, are you willing to get uncomfortable now to get comfortable later?

For me, becoming a yoga teacher helped me start connecting to myself and my voice. Nothing new can happen if you are not willing to be a partner in creating it, so steer clear of the path of least resistance for it cannot support your long-term goals and dreams. You will actually find you will flow much more easily toward your destination when you take well-planned risks and actions.

Growth and transformation do not happen without change. They happen when change occurs, and you can shift your perspective and your thinking and start fresh. If you want to get to point F, you may have to go through point B, C, D, and E first. That is where the willingness has to be strong and the commitment has to be solid. It's your path and your job to get there. Of course, you cannot do it alone. We all need each other to win in this life. But you are the seeker and the creator in your life. It's your job to find your inside healing and clear your path.

Be a seeker so you can better navigate your own life. To get to the other side, there is internal work to be done. There is pain to extract and forgiveness to give. As I mentioned earlier, as you forgive others, you are also forgiving yourself. You are peeling away the layers of shame, guilt, hurt, and pain and creating more peace, love, and light in your own life. Everyone and everything is connected and therefore your healing is a victory to all!

As you learn to get uncomfortable and release and forgive, you are freeing yourself to live the life you desire. You start finding the compassion for others that you want for yourself. You start moving closer to your goals and dreams. You realize the only thing you can control always is your own self. All that you seek is there already within you, ready to open and unfold. The more you chip away at those old layers, the faster you can break yourself free. Keep chipping away—"waxing on and waxing off"—and know you are supported, important, and loved. You *will* uncover your deeper purpose when you do the work each day.

Our actions help us create the
tomorrow we want to wake up in.

28. Never Settle for Less Than You Want

*I know I deserve to live a life full of
love and light. I am responsible to love
myself more and believe in me.*

I remember being in my twenties and sitting in the living room of my parents' house. They had their friends over, a couple who had been married for many years. I was speaking with them about life, marriage, and about what I was looking for in a partner. They were very open with me about their marriage, and the fact that they were not right for each other. However, they said, on the roller coaster of life, they would rather sit next to someone than sit alone. I told them I did not understand that because for me, it seemed very clear that, on the roller coaster of life, I would rather be alone than sit next to the wrong person. I was never going to settle for the wrong connection or relationship. I remember thinking, *Why would anyone settle for a mediocre relationship in life?*

I wanted to be happy, loved, and fulfilled in my everyday life. I did not grow up in a home where love was present between my parents, but I knew in my heart and soul that it did not have to be this way for me. This couple I was speaking with were both such amazing people, well educated, and successful in their lives. There was no reason for either one of them not to be fulfilled or happy with their choice of a life partner. No, settling would never be an option for me! It was as clear as day or night, black or white.

I also remember another informative instance in my teenage life. I used to babysit a lot, and one particular couple whose kids I cared for fascinated me. I would always catch them out of the corner of my eye being affectionate and loving toward one another. They would hug and kiss every opportunity they got. This was new and strange to me at first, but at the same time, I also loved and admired the love between them. It just seemed so easy and right. Looking at them, I knew love was possible at all times.

Everything is possible if you believe it is and if you don't settle for less than what you think you deserve in life. The problem is that too many of us settle for less just because it is there now. We really believe that we are only allowed to have certain things and therefore we put limits on ourselves and our options. We believe that our happiness is limited, our love is limited, our abundance is limited, and therefore we create a limited life that does not support us being completely loved, abundant, and self-expressed in the world.

What if you believed in no limitations and realized your own power today? How much happier and more fulfilled would you be in your life? It is your journey, your decisions, your hopes and dreams that you are responsible for creating. It all comes back to your own self-respect and self-love. Are you treating yourself with the utmost respect and love? If you are not, how can you realize that you, and only you, yourself, are creating a pattern of self-suffering and self-sabotage?

That is your work: to set boundaries for yourself and high expectations that should *never* be compromised. You must stand up for yourself, for you create your story and your happiness. When you give away your control to others, you become your own victim, even as you blame them for your suffering. That is why the power of choice is the most important aspect to focus on today. You don't have to settle; you should never settle. You get to choose your path and therefore choose your future life.

Abandon the place of scarcity and fear, and come from a place of faith and trust. Trust that when it is right, you will know it with every part of your being. It will be clear as day with an easy flow of energy, love, and light, and you will experience certainty and ease in your everyday life. You will feel supported and loved by your partner and never have to second-guess their intentions or their love. The more in sync you are with each other and the more you have in common, the easier your relationship and life will flow.

There is no reason to settle for anything less than what you want in this lifetime. Again, it goes back to eliminating those things you don't want. It is never too late, even if you are currently married to the wrong person. You can still change your life at any time if you believe in and love yourself. I know it may seem scary and impossible at times, but this is just a story you tell yourself and believe.

Like anything you want to succeed in, the first step toward success is to make a plan of action to start creating all you want. Your plan will support you in creating a new possibility in your life that was not there before. It is your job to re-create what you want and eliminate what you don't. The universe/God will support you as soon as you start supporting yourself. You will not be able to create a new life until you can stop living in that old story that keeps you powerless and a victim of your past choices in the present moment. Realizing that you want and deserve a better future and creating a new possibility for your life takes new thinking, but that is where transformation starts to happen.

One example of how to structure an action plan is to set a deadline for your goals and then work backward, outlining specific steps to get you there. The deadline you set will keep you focused and intentional on achieving your goal.

The past can never give you the life you want, but the present moment/future is wide open and ready to help you create all that you desire. You must believe everything is possible. It is not being selfish to choose to take a different direction in your life, and no one else can do it for you. Your happiness is your responsibility alone; no one can change your future but you.

When I was in my twenties and looking for my future husband, my sister said something that has always stuck with me: "Just because you love someone does not mean you should marry them." There are so many more important aspects that go into a long-lasting relationship than just love. There has to be a strong foundation to build upon for a powerful life together. Love alone doesn't always carry us through the ups and downs of life. There has to be mutual respect, friendship, and a soul connection that goes even deeper than love.

I always knew there was a fine line between love and hate; we could love somebody one day and find ourselves disliking them later. The soul connection, however, goes beyond just the physical body and what you see at this moment. It is an energy connection and exchange between the two of you, between two souls who really love each other on an energetic level: *adore*. When you find it, you will know, because it will feel like the safest place in the world. You must be 100 percent selfish when looking for your soul mate. It is not selfish to be selfish; it is a way of protecting yourself, sticking to your desires, and not settling for less. Once you find your soul mate and you know they are the person you will be spending your life with, then it is important to be selfless.

You get to create the rules in the game of your life. Take control of yourself first and make a plan to move forward today. You are not stuck, but your thoughts may be. Soon you will see new doors and opportunities that you had never seen before open up to you. You become present to the magic and grateful for every obstacle and opportunity to become who you are truly meant to be.

29. Connecting to Your Abundance

Speak kindly to yourself, for what you say becomes the light or the obstacles on your path.

There are so many people in the world who are abundant, and there is really no difference between you and them. The only difference is the separation you create in your mind.

What lets one person have so much abundance and freedom and another seem to have so little, living in a place of scarcity? Is it an education or degree? That can't be the truth because there are many high-school dropouts who are extremely successful and rich. You, therefore, must look deeper into your own life and uncover the real reason you are still thinking and playing small. You must get out of the victim mentality you have been living in and the limits you have put on yourself. Limits that have most likely been passed down to you from your family and many generations before. You must change what you have been doing and remove your own limiting personal beliefs that keep you stuck in that story from your past to create a new result: *abundance*.

Your life can only shift when you shift your thinking from scarcity to abundance. The universe is abundant and full of everything you could ever want or need. However, if you are stuck in the scarcity story, there is no room for you to receive the abundance the universe/God has to offer you. You see, the doors of scarcity are empty like a dry desert, with very little energy flowing toward you and your life. Yet the doors of abundance are wide open with a constant flow of energy moving toward you. It is important to notice which door you are more connected to. You must first believe that you deserve all of the abundance and energy you want to flow into your life. You do that by changing the focus of your thoughts from scarcity to abundance (even though you can't see it at this very moment but trusting that it is there waiting to be uncovered). I used to imagine myself in a room filled with gold and jewels. All I had to do was reach out and grab them.

What would you have to give up to start connecting to that flow of abundance in your life? Would you have to give up the limited beliefs of others? Would you have to let go of people who don't see your true potential? Would you have to stop listening to the opinions of certain friends and family members? Would you need to sit down and start creating on paper a new story that inspires you or an image of the life that you would love to live? Would you have to be more intentional with your time and follow through? Would you have to stop doing the same old thing and expect a new result?

In this case, you must think outside the box, creating totally fresh and new ways to see and experience your life. One step at a time, you will start seeing real opportunities open up for you. As you start changing your thinking, you are creating new openings of energy flowing toward you to start the process of shifting and changing your life. The universe starts aligning with your words and actions and starts pulling you toward the things you desire most.

It is a simple formula, so why is it so difficult to execute? If you cannot do this, it is because you were conditioned at a very early age to see things a certain way. Your conditioning is so strong that you even use the same disempowering words over and over again that have been running your life up to now. The words you choose are hurting your future, your happiness, your abundance, your health, and your well-being without your full awareness. Your connection to those words will affect you daily.

If you keep saying life will be hard, then life will be hard. If you keep saying your kids are impossible, you will be right, and they will show up as difficult, just like you said. *Everything* is a reflection of your words at this very moment.

Your change will mirror a change in the universe and in all your current situations. This is your work, to start seeing that you must mirror what you want. It is that constant commitment to yourself that will keep you connected to joy, abundance, and happiness in your life.

30. A Guideline to Change

*The journey is always there to
help us uncover the miracles of life.
Every setback is a chance for self-connection,
compassion, re-creation, and love. All is
working perfectly in my life and I am grateful.*

If you are ready to create change and start living the life you desire, answer the following questions in a journal or notebook, being as specific as possible.

1. What area of your life are you committed to change?

2. What is NOT working in that area?

3. What do you need and want to create in that area?

4. How can you stay focused on creating your goal?

5. What might you need to eliminate in your life to get what you desire?

6. Write an action plan on how to move forward. Be really detailed, focused, and intentional with what you want.

7. What boundaries do you need to set so you can move more easily toward your goal? These boundaries are essential to stay focused and avoid distractions.

8. Who can support you to reach your goal?

   For example, if you are in an unfulfilling partnership or relationship, your steps might be

1. **Goal:** Find my soul mate or life partner.

2. **Not Working:** No connection, no love, no desire, no commitment, no romance.

3. **Need and Want:** Friendship, unconditional love, adoration, commitment, trust.

4. **How:** Don't settle. Stay true to yourself. Love yourself first.

5. **Eliminate:** The wrong people, small talk, empty promises, compromise.

6. **Plan:** Don't waste time with the wrong people—be honest and open about what you want and expect others to do the same. Eliminate quickly the wrong ones so that you can get to the right one.

7. **Boundaries:** With open communication, let others know your expectations, and never settle for less than you deserve and want. Boundaries and expectations should be set at the beginning of every encounter or potential relationship. Never be afraid to be you!

8. **Support:** Let friends and people you encounter know that you are looking for a partner. Don't be afraid to spread the word. People love to help others find love!

31. The Gift of Your Body

Your body is a onetime gift; take care of your body so that your body can take care of you.

I cannot overemphasize how important it is for you to take care of your body and yourself. Most of us were blessed to be born healthy with a healthy body to live in. Having the freedom to move your body feels great and is a true blessing and gift. It really is such a miracle that most of us take for granted daily. Your body is your temple, your happiness, your source of self-love. This is where the breath flows, energy moves effortlessly, and life exists. How blessed are you to have the honor of living in your body! Commit to nurturing and taking care of it to maintain its longevity daily.

What you do today determines what body you will have tomorrow. Knowing that my body was a one-time gift and that I was not going to get a new one in this lifetime, I was committed to maintaining its longevity. I realized that being in the sun too much was not good for my youthful skin. I was also aware of the effect of smoking on my skin, aging, and well-being. I realized alcohol and drugs were not good for my body and mind, and what I ate and put in my body really mattered. I am very grateful that I have compassion for and self-awareness of my body.

I am so thankful to have a body that works for me and not against me. Just look around at the elderly; so many of them are trapped in bodies that no longer work for them, but rather work against them. I can think of nothing worse than being trapped in your own body, having to depend on others for mobility and well-being.

You must invest in your health and well-being today because there is nothing more important than you. It really is a choice and a commitment to yourself. You cannot take care of anyone else if you do not take care of yourself first. What you choose to eat becomes who you are, so be mindful and careful of the choices you make. It is entirely up to you to choose your path of health, for you are the creator of your healthy life.

You can always re-create yourself by breaking an old cycle and creating a new one by setting new intentions and putting actions in place that support them in your life. Be inspired by you, love yourself, and take care of yourself—no one else can do it for you! Eat nutritious foods that help energize your body and your life. Stay away from manufactured processed foods; they will never give you the health and well-being you are seeking.

Find people to teach you and support you so cooking healthily and eating healthy is always an option. Be open to trying new foods; it's never too late to get a fresh start. You will feel as good on the inside as you look on the outside. Enjoy what you eat and feel good. My body thanks me every day for feeding it healthy and nourishing foods.

Here are some steps for taking care of your body and yourself:

1. Accept yourself fully as you are right now. The most important thing is to love yourself because without love no change can happen. Self-love always first! Choose to be more conscious about what you are eating and drinking. Food is the energy that helps you become who you are. I recommend an organic plant-based diet full of vitamins and minerals. Stay away from man-made food, for it's dead and has no real nutritional value. When you love yourself, you nurture your mind, body, and soul. I believe in choosing organic fruits and vegetables for a healthy diet, and avoiding processed, manufactured foods that are hard to digest.

2. Remember, your body is composed mostly of water, so be sure to drink plenty of filtered water every day.

3. Take care of your body by not smoking, drinking, or doing drugs, as they have long-term negative effects on your body, mind, and spirit.

4. Take care of your skin. Use sunblock every day to protect it and keep it from prematurely aging. Put only natural, plant-based products on your skin because it is your largest organ and absorbs virtually everything into your bloodstream.

5. Fill yourself with positive thoughts and focus on positive outcomes.

6. Exercise regularly to stay flexible, limber, strong, and healthy. The body needs movement—my trainer recommends I get at least 30 minutes of cardio daily.

7. Get annual physicals, health screenings, dental cleanings and exams, and limit or eliminate unnecessary pharmaceutical drugs by choosing natural alternatives.

8. Replace unhealthy foods with healthier food options. No need to ever starve yourself or diet! Finding healthy foods you love is the key to changing your eating habits and waist size.

Make yourself the biggest project to work on daily. You deserve to fill yourself with unconditional love and light. You can only give what is already inside you.

32. What to Look for in a Soul Mate

On the roller coaster of life, I would rather be alone than sitting with the wrong person.

As I mentioned earlier, when I was dating a man my younger sister thought would not be the appropriate choice as a husband for me, she gave me one of the wisest pieces of advice I've ever received. She said, "Just because you love someone does not mean you should marry them."

"But I love him," I protested.

"Love is not enough for a long-lasting life together," she replied.

This made me stop and think and look deeper into the choices I was making.

What are you really looking for in a soul mate? You must first be really clear about what it is you want. Having common values is most important. Opposites may attract, but they don't necessarily last for a lifetime. Sometimes the very things you are attracted to when you are dating someone are the very things you may despise later. For example, a man who is always in charge and taking care of every detail when you are dating may actually wind up being controlling when you marry him. In dating, it may be attractive to have him take the lead in life, but in a marriage, it may be suffocating, and you may be miserable. The very thing you thought you loved can become the very thing you resent or even hate later.

As I said earlier, there is actually a very fine line between love and hate, and maybe that is why the divorce rate is so high today. Get clear about what you love about the person you're with. Is it their caring heart and listening ear? Or is what you love the fact that they are fun and adventurous? You must learn to look deeper into the soul of the person you are choosing, not the surface layer of who they are.

When I walked down the aisle at my wedding, I knew I was marrying "the most wonderful man in the world." I loved his heart and soul, and we had a deep connection with each other. I did not need to guess how he felt because he was always open to share it with me. He is my best friend. Twenty-two years later, our connection is even stronger than it was back then, and I am blessed to spend my life with such a beautiful partner and soul.

It is important to keep your eyes wide open. The most important things to look for in a soul mate, starting from their core and closest connections and working your way out, are:

1. Is he or she your best friend?

2. How stable was their childhood? How did they grow up, and how stable are they now?

3. Do they love the members of their family? Are they close?

4. Was there constant stability in their early life? Did they have good role models of what parents, grandparents, or mentors should be?

5. Have they worked through their traumas and issues? If so, what did they do to create a change in their life?

6. Are they flexible, open, easygoing, and loving?

7. Do they have potential for success in their life?

8. Do they show they adore you, not with words but with actions?

9. Are they open with their communication?

10. Are they there for you when you need them most?

11. Do their words align with their actions?

12. Do you have a good physical connection?

13. Are you choosing with your heart and your feelings, or are you choosing with your head?

14. Are you making sure you eliminate the wrong people in your life to find your soul mate?

15. Do you flow easily together—no roller-coaster ride?

16. Are your souls connected?

Remember:

❣ Always choose with your head. That's why your head is above your heart.

- Elimination is the key. The faster you eliminate the wrong ones, the faster you will reach your soul mate. Make it a game, have fun, and don't be disappointed; most people will not be the one, so don't invest in them.

- Don't wear your heart on your sleeve. Never give someone your heart before they show you they deserve it with their actions, not their words. Words are cheap and weak if they are not rooted in actions!

- Everyone you meet and date is a chance to make new friends and connections, and maybe they will even lead you to the one.

- You can never say the wrong thing to the right person.

LET SELF-LOVE BE YOUR GUIDE

I cannot overemphasize the importance of being mindful in your choice of a partner. I see it as the foundation to a beautiful and fulfilling life full of joy, peace, and happiness. For instance, when I walked down the aisle, I knew I was marrying a truly beautiful soul and the most wonderful man in the world. Please don't rush into love before giving yourself permission to love yourself first. Let your own self-acceptance and self-love be your guide! The right partner will always come from love and show you support. That person will be your biggest cheerleader in life, and you will be theirs. They will be the wind beneath your wings and together you will fly higher than you ever imagined is possible!

33. Changing Old Patterns with Self-Love and Compassion

Find the peace within yourself and
you will be a source of peace for the world.

Only when you have self-love and compassion for yourself can you have it for others in your life. Only when you learn to judge yourself less can you be less judgmental and more accepting of others. Everything always comes back to you, since you are the force that drives everything in your own life. Your responsibility is, first and foremost, to yourself, before anyone else. And no, it is not selfish, but important and necessary. How can you be a source of water for others if your well is completely dry? How can you give to others if you are completely depleted yourself?

Like they say on airplanes, in case of emergency, first put on your mask, then help your kids put theirs on. Any other way would be detrimental to the health and well-being of your life and future as well as theirs. You are the very foundation upon which everything in your life grows and evolves. The foundation has to be strong, yet well nurtured and happy, to live a well-balanced and fulfilling life. How do you find that unconditional acceptance and love for your own existence first?

My yoga teacher, Terri Cooper, had a T-shirt made that read "Hurt people hurt people." It's sad, but in most cases, this is so true. How can you do better if you have never learned how to be kind and compassionate toward yourself? As I've mentioned previously, you only know what you saw growing up, and usually your way of being is a product of your past experiences. I truly believe most people would do better if they only knew how and had the tools they needed.

How can you shift and change those old patterns that have been so ingrained in you for so many years? It takes lots and lots of self-forgiveness first, as well as acceptance of where you are right now. Years of conditioning sometimes takes years to shift and change. It comes down to whether you are willing to be open and patient with yourself in the now, meeting yourself exactly where you are with compassion and love for yourself and your life.

Here are some things to remember and think about:

❣ When you start to realize the connection in every aspect of your life, you can be more forgiving to yourself and to others. You learn to let go of those things that are not giving you the peace and love you so desire in your life today. Slowly you start reconnecting to yourself and getting a better understanding of why you are the way you are today. You learn to stop rejecting your own dark side and instead accept it by shining your light on it. Be accepting right now, know that transformation can only take place with your acceptance, compassion, and love.

❣ Whatever you resist persists. If you are truly ready for change, you cannot keep resisting yourself, but rather you must meet yourself right where you are, with love in your heart and compassion in your soul.

❣ How do you fill your cup daily with love and compassion? You cannot pour from an empty cup. In other words, you cannot give it if you do not have it. You need to fill your cup by bringing more compassion to yourself, by being more present and noticing how you nurture yourself, and speak to yourself, so you can fill your mind, body, and soul.

❣ Are you constantly comparing yourself or competing with others, or are you content and grateful in your life? Gratitude is the one constant forward flow.

❣ Treat yourself the way you would want others to treat you, and stop beating yourself up for your past mistakes by realizing everything is here at the right time to support your growth and transformation. There are no mistakes, just lessons! Be grateful for this moment of consciousness and growth within which you want to do better, be better, and grow.

❣ Notice the old stories that are still keeping you stuck, making you a victim in your own head and therefore in your life. Realize you and only you have the power to transform hate to love and anger to peace.

❣ The only way to re-create is to accept and forgive with love and compassion, understanding that you are human and having love and compassion for your own humanity is an important key to your healing. Learn to pause, breathe, feel, and connect to your own essence and being, since all change is within you. Love and compassion are a gift you give yourself, ones that no one can take away from you. Listen to yourself and pour love on yourself always.

❣ When negative judgments and thoughts come into your head, tell them, "Thank you for sharing, but I know this is not the truth." Learn to let them go as fast as they come into your space. That is taking back your own power and not being stuck in negativity!

❣ Are you in touch with yourself, your needs, and your self-care? Are you taking the time to get proper sleep at night in order to feel recharged during the day? Are you choosing to feed your body with healthy fruits and vegetables to help your body flow better? Are you scheduling daily time to fill your cup with love through yoga, meditation, reading, writing, exercising, friends, massage, and relaxation, or anything that lifts your heart and nourishes your soul? If not, start today for every moment is a chance for a new beginning!

Living a more mindful and purposeful life that awakens your soul and spirit daily is your work and your work alone. As your heart expands and opens, you can then have more room to share that love and compassion in the world. Your transformation is everyone's transformation. You become a light for others to follow their own paths and love their own lives. Don't speak negatively about your life; learn to speak only with kindness, truth, faith, and hope to create your most inspirational life.

34. Ten Things to Let Go So You Can Grow

Eliminate what is not working
in order to create the life you love.

You must learn to let go of certain things to free yourself from yourself. Your limited beliefs and opinions can keep you hostage in your own life. You see things only as you know them, not necessarily from a fresh perspective and outlook. As you peel back the layers of your life, you get closer to the purpose of your soul's journey. You open up a clearing for fresh opportunities ahead. You start seeing life through a fresh lens, no longer burdened by the heaviness of your past. You are able to create new opportunities for yourself that were not possible before.

Here are ten things you can start to let go of today to lift your soul and spirit.

1. Let go of trying to control everything and everyone.
No one likes to be controlled, not even you. When you feel you are being controlled, you resist and fight back. It leaves you feeling sad, disempowered, and uninspired. Rather than trying to control people and eliciting these same responses in them, lead by example. Be an

inspiring teacher others may wish to follow through your words and actions. Learn to trust what is and let go of what isn't. Learn to surrender to the flow of your life. The only person you want to control is yourself.

2. **Let go of being right and making others wrong.** When you are right, it may make you feel good for the moment, but at what cost to others? Being right all the time does not create a happy and fulfilling life for you or the people around you. It isolates you and can make you be and feel alone. On the other hand, allowing others to be right does not make you wrong; it creates connections. It releases the ego, and lets you be right as well. You leave others feeling good about themselves and empowered, which in turn empowers you and makes you feel good about yourself. It's a win-win situation and comes from a place of connection, caring, and love.

3. **Let go of comparison of and competition with others.** Know that there is no scarcity, only the scarcity you create in your own mind. We are all unique. There is no need to compare or compete with anyone else! You hold a unique life message and gifts to spread in the world. Competition and comparison will truly disconnect you from creating your greenest grass and best life. By giving up comparison, you will find a deeper connection to yourself, others, and life. When you support others, others will support you. Whatever energy you put into the world comes back to you ten-fold. Always be happy for others and wish them the best on their journey. Since we are all connected, none of us can win without each other's love and support.

We must learn to support one another rather than try to compete against one another in this lifetime.

4. **Let go of the idea that you don't have everything you need.** You do! All you have to do is believe and start taking little actions toward your goals. The universe/God always opens its doors for you when you are ready to start creating your dreams. You know what you need to know right now, and you will learn more as you move forward on your journey. Like Dorothy in *The Wizard of Oz*, you have all you need inside you to return home to yourself. As you peel away the layers of your life that are weighing you down by eliminating and renewing, you discover that anything is possible right now if you believe.

5. **Let go of living your life without realizing your impact on others.** Everything you do has an impact on something or someone. Being aware of your impact is important for you to grow and bring more consciousness into your life. When you live your life unaware of your impact, you keep creating obstacles for yourself without realizing that you are doing so. Everything and anything you do out there in the world is reflected back at you like a mirror and creates your reality now. Learn to take notice of your impact and be responsible for your actions. This is crucial to your forward movement growth and development of what you want to create.

6. **Let go of making a big deal out of every little thing.** Whenever you get stuck on something small, it robs you of your happiness, love, and light. Release little

annoyances so that you can flow with life moment by moment. Release any old habits of getting fixated on minutia. Realize that you can learn to control your emotions and choose a happier path. Can you be okay when things don't go exactly your way? For example, if you order food and it isn't exactly how you wanted it to be, can you accept this without clinging to disappointment? Can you not make a big deal out of it? Can you learn to let it go so you can flow? Find a solution instead without the upset. It is up to you at every moment to make that decision and not get stuck on the little things life throws your way.

7. **Let go of taking things for granted and be grateful for everything.** Learn to be grateful for the smallest things you take for granted and see them as miracles in your life. Having eyes to see and legs to walk are a couple of things to be grateful for. Everything we enjoy today was a gift from someone before. They are so important but easy to take for granted. The beauty of our differences is another thing to be grateful for, as life would be boring if we were all the same. Don't be jealous or envious. Be grateful for other people's gifts, for they can make your life better with their contributions to you and the world. Being thankful for your lifetime in general and the small yet irreplaceable miracles you enjoy every day will bring you happiness and joy.

8. **Let go of taking life so seriously and making it so heavy.** Laughing at yourself and with others, having fun and dancing through life is your choice. Give yourself permission to create joy, peace, and happiness

that you deserve to have, realizing you have the power to re-create yourself at every moment and at any time. You are the driver of your life. A great example of this for me is my greatest teacher, my husband, Steven. He dances through life. He wakes up every day happy and excited, with a fresh outlook on life. He is not weighed down by what happens to him during the day at work, and he always has a big smile on his face and joy in his heart. It truly is contagious and to be around him is a joy and honor. He does not care who is around no matter where we are; he will just hug me or kiss me freely, with no restraints, which really is a beautiful thing to experience. He has created that freedom of self-expression within himself and his life. He is no longer controlled by society or others. I admire who he is, and I am blessed to be on this journey together. It is up to you to set yourself free and stop carrying the heaviness of yesterday with you daily.

9. **Let go of judgment.** When you learn to separate yourself from your judgments, you realize they are not always the truth. Judgments on some levels keep us separated from others. There is freedom in releasing our judgments, for it creates more connection and self-acceptance of ourselves and others. The more we judge others, the harder we are on ourselves, too.

10. **Let go of drama and chaos.** There is plenty of drama and chaos in life without creating it ourselves! Stay away from gossip and toxic relationships. Learn from them instead to create more peace in your future. Choose wisely who you surround yourself with.

35. Your Words and Affirmations Will Change Your Truth

Our words create our world,
and our world is created by our words.

Notice what you say to yourself and write it down. Awareness is the first step to change. When you find yourself saying things that are negative, like negative self-talk, notice it, and say, "Cancel," then re-create it with a positive affirmation. For example, if you say to yourself, "My kids are always late to school and are not responsible," change this to "My kids care about learning and will always be on time for school because they are responsible." Another example, if you keep telling yourself, "Life is hard and I am drowning," change this to "I am always supported and loved in my life."

Use a journal to write what you are creating in the present tense as though it is happening right now. An example of that could be, "I have my dream job, and everything I want is coming easily toward me." Be open to receive and know there is more out there than you can see right now. Remember, our vision as human beings is limited, and we usually do not see the whole picture at this time. So put out there what you want to receive. Do kind things if you want to receive the kindness of the world. Be in your authentic truth; your authentic truth will attract love and light more easily into your life. Whatever you put out, you will receive back in one form or another, so be mindful of what you are drawing toward you. Have faith and trust that the universe/God or your higher power is always supporting your life and path.

Here are some examples of changing your self-talk:

❧ "I am awkward," change to "I am unique and loved and accepted by all."

❧ "I am weak," change to "I am capable, smart, strong and powerful."

❧ "I am poor," change to "I am rich and abundant. I have all I need right now."

❧ "I am stressed," change to "I am grateful."

❧ "I am bored with life," change to "I am excited to create all I want."

❧ "I am confused," change to "I am intentional with my path and my direction."

❧ "Life is hard," change to "I am powerful and capable."

❧ "I am alone," change to "I am supported, guided, and loved as I walk through my journey."

36. Get Excited About Your Life

*Being fully self-expressed in my life lets me
paint the world in many different colors.*

My coach Ed Bohlke said to me that if I am not excited about my life, I am not grateful either. I did not understand it at first because I always saw myself as grateful, but I definitely was not always excited and my energy was low most days. Why was I not excited? Why did I see life as heavy and overwhelming at times? Why was it so hard for me to wake up in the morning and be excited about my life and my day?

Realizing there is more self-work to be done and layers to remove is a never-ending part of growth and transformation—to learn to live more intentionally in daily life will raise your energy and excitement.

Are you present to the miracle of being alive each day? Present to the beautiful members of your family? Are you excited to see and be with them daily? Or are you resisting them by not making them a priority or ignoring them and therefore your own happiness in life suffers? Can you give up your own deep-rooted resistance to find a new aliveness and excitement for your life? That's how deeply we must learn to look at ourselves to raise our vibration and energize our life.

Excitement is so contagious, and when you are excited, you awaken excitement in everyone around you. Your excitement will reignite feelings of passion, which will inspire others to get excited about their own lives. By raising your vibrational energy, you get to release the bondage of mediocrity from your life and therefore elevate your life. It all has to do with where your mental state is at at all times, which is up to you to control.

Be more aware of the people and energy you want to attract toward you. You can get excited over the smallest things in life because those things are really the biggest gifts of life. Get excited now about your health, your kids, your partner, your goals, and your dreams. Start describing in detail all that you appreciate and love about them. See life in beautiful, vivid colors. Let the special people in your life know how grateful you are for them and how priceless their presence in your life is.

Awaken your mind, body, and spirit, allowing that excitement to flow back into your life. Find passion once again for what has been numb or unawakened for too long now. This is a method of injecting more light and love into your life. Dance, sing, and play—life is beautiful when you stop resisting and surrender to the beat of your soul.

37. At the End, What Will Be Most Important to You?

*My life is a gift and I treat it that way,
as I choose to focus on what is going
to be most important at the end.*

As I mentioned earlier in this book, I think about the end of my life and work backward to today to remind myself of what is truly important to me in this lifetime. At the end of my life, what will be most important to me will not be things I acquired, like the car I drove or the jewelry I owned, but rather the people I loved most—my family, my friends, animal companions, and so on—and the love and light I created intentionally in my life. These are things money could never buy.

My heart is always filled with gratitude when I am focused on what really counts. I no longer let little and small things that are not as important and replaceable become the center of my happiness in my life.

I encourage you to do this as well. Think about your final moments and ask yourself if you have taken anything for granted. Have you focused on the gifts that really count, like health, happiness, joy, and love? This is the awareness you need to bring into today and focus on what really counts right now. When you do this, you will stop allowing the small, replaceable things to become your happiness or define who you are.

See the gift of your greenest grass surrounding you when you are present in your life. There is always so much to be grateful and thankful for. Look deeper inside yourself to connect to your heart and to the love you desire. It's love for you as well as for others that is deeply rooted and gives you a meaningful life.

We are born in a moment and die in a moment, but what's most important is what we do with all those moments in between.

You Are Greater Than You Think!

Be grateful for all that you are, all that you are becoming, and all that you will be. We are here for a reason: Let's keep moving forward.

My wish for you is that you realize your true potential in this life. You are greater than you may have previously thought. As I've explained throughout this book, years of lack of intention and focus on what you want may have blinded you from seeing that truth. Perhaps a childhood in which you were put down, bullied, had no direction, experienced traumas, and did not learn self-control has contributed to your inability to see your greatness now. Whatever the reason for feelings of disempowerment, a wall of shame, hurt, guilt, and disappointment resulted. Perhaps you have been caught in a cycle of self-abuse or maybe you are unable to push self-limiting beliefs aside and start anew. It does not have to be this way. The power to grow, change, and transform is yours always.

Maybe you are like I was. In my case, a lack of focus and intention coupled with fear kept me doing everything but being with myself. I did not like myself. I constantly looked for others to give me the reassurance and love I could not give myself. How could I share my message with others if I could not bear to spend time with myself? In my thoughts and dreams, someday I would be somebody I would be proud of. In reality, I knew that I was dreaming rather than creating a life of fulfillment and self-empowerment.

Yes, my life was working now, and I felt happier than I had ever been. Yet the problem was not with what was going on outside me. Years of sadness and pain were still at the core of my being. The emotions were stuck in my body, and energetically I could not shake them out. Everything on the outside seemed great, yet everything on the inside was still broken. I wanted to leap out and run away from the old me, yet the old me was still the new me. It was all connected, and the problem was my own disconnection between the two. I discovered that my greenest grass wasn't somewhere in the future. It was exactly where I was standing right now.

I knew I was born with a message that could change people's lives because it had changed my own. I did not want to leave this earth without giving this message to the world. I kept watch to see if anyone else had that same message, and I realized fifteen years later that it was my unique gift to the world. "The Grass Is Greenest Where I Am" was and is my piece, my contribution, my message to share with you.

You have an important message to share and contribute to this world, too. You count, and your message is unique and important. Your past may help you create your message like mine did. How can you find strength from your past to reshape your future? That's your work here, today, to take all the suffering and turn it into growth and strength in your life. To do that, start with acceptance and forgiveness for your past and notice that your grass is greenest wherever you are standing right now. Do the deep emotional work required to help you release yourself from past traumas that may be holding you back. It takes real commitment to yourself and your life to learn how to balance energies in your own body. It's being committed to peeling away those layers and old stories so you can write a new story that empowers you. The work is deeper than you may realize and can be very confronting, but, in your heart, you will know there is healing on the other side.

I could not have sat down long enough to write a sentence, let alone a book, until I did my own deep work. You are me, and I am you. Whatever you see in me is in you, too. If I did it, I promise you that you can do it for sure.

Always remember that giving up is not an option. The solution is there; you just need to keep your eye on the ball and keep moving forward with your actions. The reward of living a life you love is priceless. This is an investment in you, and the doors to all that you ever wanted and desired will open when you do your work. Don't let fear stop you once again, for it will freeze your life and keep you from knowing yourself fully. There are so many resources out there to support you, like Landmark Education, books, therapists, chakra work, meditation, hypnosis, and so on. Get out of your head, reach out to others, and start building a life you love. Why not you? This is your time to rise and shine and fulfill the purpose you were born for.

The Greenest Grass Meditation

As we deepen our breath, we calm our mind so that we can find a connection to this moment with gratitude and love.

Meditation gives you a chance to plug into your inner world and unplug from your outer world. You will find a connection to your breath and a connection to yourself. You can let go of attachment to the physical self with all its wants and desires. You learn to connect to your soul and your essence.

How do you find balance between such different worlds? How do you stay connected in the physical world where life is coming at you so fast? That is the work and that is the freedom you can find through meditation. You will become aware that your inner world is actually a reflection of your outer world and that your outer world is the reflection of your inner world. As you find the connection in yourself, and you start creating harmony between those two worlds, you will find balance and connection in all aspects of yourself and your life.

As you do your work, you get to put the pieces of your

life together from the inside out. You learn to forgive, to let go, to accept, to love, to be present, and to be kind to yourself and others. As that inner world becomes healed, you create a full circle of light that your outer world will reflect and mirror. You will create a wholeness in yourself that contributes to the life and wholeness of others. Together we are "won."

GREENEST GRASS MEDITATION

Note: *For a free download of this meditation, visit www. noahcrane.com.*

1. Sit in an easy cross-legged position, nice and tall, close your eyes, and let your arms rest comfortably on your lap, or find any comfortable position.

2. As you root your feet into the floor, lengthen your spine as you reach the crown of your head toward the ceiling or sky.

3. Find connection to this moment, to the earth, to your breath, and to your life.

4. Relax your shoulders and let your shoulder blades melt down your back.

5. Just breathe. Inhale deeply through your nose and exhale through your mouth.

6. With every inhale, drop your diaphragm and expand your chest.

7. With every exhale, lift your diaphragm way up.

8. Bring your focus to your third eye, that space between your eyebrows, and deepen your breath.

9. Your breath is flowing easily through you. You are grounded in yourself and in this moment in your life. Feel the earth beneath you and know that you are supported, loved, and guided on your journey.

10. Now, imagine a stream of water. Watch the water flow. Observe the water moving past any rocks and obstacles in its way. Realize that water is always moving forward somehow, no matter what is going on.

11. As you observe the water, start realizing the connection of water to your breath. See that the water is flowing easily down with no effort and so is your breath. How interesting to find connection in totally different aspects of life.

12. A smile comes across your face as you realize the power of connections. Breath flows, water flows, moments flow, days flow, years flow—everything flows at all times.

13. What are some of the obstacles or experiences that keep you from flowing forward? What is holding you back in your life now? Is it old heartache? Old fears of not being good enough? Is it fear of your true power and greatness?

14. You realize nothing stays the same, and you want to stay connected to that flow as well, the flow of life, the flow of breath, the flow of water.

15. You realize you are also ready to flow forward as you observe how good it feels to release things that no longer serve you and are stopping your forward movement and flow. It may be time to let them go and surrender to love.

16. Reconnect to friends and family, and be more centered in yourself. It may be time to let go of old resentments and fears, those things that are stopping your forward movement and flow now.

17. Realize you have a choice every day and at every moment to re-create a life you love. It is your time now. It is a time for shift and change, a time to let go of all the old stories that are keeping you stuck in your past and to release all doubt and fears that are keeping you frozen in your life today.

18. Bring your hands to your heart. Notice a sensation that is there, that sensation of joy, that sensation of love, that is always within you.

19. Bring your palms together at your heart center, and gently bow to yourself. You feel renewed, grateful, and excited for the journey ahead.

20. Lie down on your mat in Savasana (the yoga "corpse pose"). Imagine the warm sun kissing your face and body. You are relaxed and peaceful now. Your heart is full of love and light.

21. Now imagine that you are floating on a raft on a calm stream of water. Life feels happy and light now as you enjoy the present moment with ease and flow. Feel

the heat of the sun kissing your face and body as the water droplets cool you off.

22. You realize anything is possible when you let go of the old stories and create a new possibility for yourself and your life. Release the limitations and barriers that are stopping your forward flow.

23. A smile comes across your face. You feel happy and free. You are grateful for connections and excited to keep flowing toward your future.

24. Bring your hands back to your heart. Feel that heart that beats only for you. Connect to this present moment with love and gratitude.

25. Say to yourself, "The Grass Is Greenest Where I Am! THE GRASS IS GREENEST WHERE I AM! I am grateful for myself and my life."

Acknowledgments

In addition to my gratitude to the universe/God, I would like to acknowledge the following people. Without their contributions, I could not have brought out my message so elegantly, thoughtfully, and thoroughly.

Steven Crane—my husband, my love, and my most ardent supporter. The grass is greenest where I am, especially since I have you in my life. I am grateful for all your love and support always.

Sima—my mom, who has supported and loved me from the bottom of her heart since the day I was born. You are an amazing mom, and I cherish every moment we get to be together. I love you with all my heart and soul.

My three amazing children—Ilan, Orry, and Tali. I am grateful for all the important lessons you taught me, and I love you very much always.

My stepfather, Jack—without whom I would not have as much material for this book. Thank you for your contribution to my life. I love you.

My sister, Ayelet—I want to thank you for being my sister and always guiding me and loving me. You are a true blessing in my life; thank you for always being there for me. Your wisdom, kindness, and generosity have inspired me to be a better person. I love you.

My brother, Shachar—Thank you for being in my life and keeping our family strong. I love you.

To my beautiful mother-in-law, Ziva Crane, now in heaven —I am forever grateful for having you in my life. You gave me your most amazing son. Thank you! I miss you and Mike so much. I will always treasure our memories together. I love you.

Denise Bordeau—Meeting you was truly a gift and a blessing. I love you and our friendship. Thank you for typing my manuscript and trusting me for guidance. You are a dear friend and I thank you for allowing me to share your inspiring story with my readers.

The Book Couple, Gary and Carol—Thank you for your friendship and also for making the process of getting my book out into the world so easy. Carol, thank you for your support in editing my book. You helped me polish it and make it sparkle. For Gary, thank you for designing my book cover and helping to get my book off the ground.

Special thanks to Conscious Co-op: Conscious Community Connection for keeping me focused on the message and creating a space where love and light are always present.

Special thanks to Kristen Noffsinger, my dear friend, closest collaborator, and the grease that makes Conscious Co-op and my social media run so smoothly.

Michele D'Ambrosio—Thank you for always being a friend and a mentor. We are always connected.

Ed Bohlke—Thank you for helping me raise my deserve level.

Joanna Francis—I am so blessed to have met you and David. Thank you for giving me great feedback on my book.

To anyone I have not named, please know that I am grateful for you and the contribution you have made to my life.

I love you all.

About the Author

Noah Crane is a life and empowerment coach, public speaker, and certified integrative nutrition counselor. She is also a 500-hour Vinyasa Flow Yoga Teacher, as well as certified in Yin Yoga and Pilates Reformer. Noah is the founder of Conscious Co-op, a group of like-minded individuals who are finding connection with a mission to awaken healing and spread love and light in the world. She created this group because she believes the power of connection is the key to all that we want to create in our lives, and says, "Together we are 'won.'"

Her focus is on empowering people to live a happy and fulfilling life. She believes in nurturing, self-care, and having love toward one's self as a daily practice. Noah is committed to helping people find their unique gifts and life purpose to leave a lasting impact on the world. Her mission is to lift souls to a higher consciousness to transcend limitations and create a life of love and light. Visit **www.noahcrane.com**.